THE HANGING
& REDEMPTION
of
JOHN GORDON

THE TRUE STORY OF
RHODE ISLAND'S LAST EXECUTION

D0064112

PAUL F. CARANCI

Charleston — London
THE
History
PRESS

Published by The History Press
Charleston, SC 29403
www.historypress.net

Copyright © 2013 by Paul F. Caranci
All rights reserved

First published 2013

Manufactured in the United States

ISBN 978.1.60949.868.9

Library of Congress CIP data applied for.

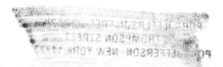

To Margie, whose love and inspiration are more apparent with each passing year, and in loving memory of my dad.

CONTENTS

CONTENTS

ACKNOWLEDGEMENTS

I express my heartfelt gratitude to the many people who provided information and inspiration to me in bringing this project to fruition. Although this book is the culmination of time spent with many people during the course of my research, I particularly want to recognize the expertise, support and encouragement of Dr. Patrick T. Conley, Representative Peter Martin, playwright Ken Dooley, public defender Michael DiLauro and North Providence town historian Thomas Greene as well as the staffs at the Rhode Island State Archives, the State Library, the Cranston Town Clerk's Office, the Rhode Island Historical Society, the Office of Statewide Planning and the Providence Public Library, where I spent countless hours scouring through old microfilm reels of nineteenth-century *Providence Journal* articles. Of particular note is the assistance of the Cranston Historical Society, especially Sandra Mayor, its president, and James Hall, the curator of the Sprague mansion, who spent hours with me providing insights and tours of the Sprague mansion, directing me through the beaten paths of Saint Ann's Cemetery and leading me to the site of the former foot bridge, the site of Amasa Sprague's murder. Finally, my thanks to Ms. Patricia Luciolla, the Unified Arts Department Chair at the North Providence High School, and the students of her Honors Visual Art in Society class for their diligence in providing cover art design. Those students—Lynnette Munoz, Stephanie Tamburrino, Eric Chidiac, Kyle Calandra—possess extraordinary talent and will surely have a promising future in the arts field.

Foreword

The earliest Native Americans of Rhode Island, the people we call "Indians," have preserved and maintained some of their culture and traditions orally, one generation to the next. Later arrivals to the area have done the same but to a lesser degree because they have relied more on the written word.

Irish Americans also have their stories and legends to transmit. One of the most persistent relates to a young Catholic immigrant who was framed and hanged for the brutal murder of a powerful, influential Yankee mill owner, Amasa Sprague of Cranston. Growing up in the largely Irish-American neighborhood of South Providence, which was a part of Cranston until 1868, I heard my family members refer to the Gordon story nearly every time a death penalty case made national headlines. "There is no death penalty in Rhode Island," I was told, "because of the martyrdom of John Gordon."

In the 1950s, when I was a teenager, the century-old antagonism between Irish Catholic Democrats and white Anglo-Saxon Protestants (called "WASPS") still simmered. It was said that an Irish American amnesiac forgot everything but his grudge against the Yankees. The memory of John Gordon contributed to the animosity between the two groups.

As the Diocese of Providence began to prepare for its centennial anniversary in 1972, future bishop Daniel Reilly of South Providence asked me and my neighborhood friend, future House Speaker Matthew Smith, to write a history of early Catholicism in Rhode Island for the observance. We complied, though belatedly. On July 6, 1973, with our book still unfinished, we published an excerpt from it about the trial of John Gordon in the *Providence Visitor*, the diocesan newspaper. This opening but very short salvo in the campaign to vindicate Gordon got little attention, even when we expanded it in our long-overdue centennial volume *Catholicism in Rhode Island: The Formative Era* (1976).

Meanwhile, my continuing research on the Dorr Rebellion revealed that some leaders of the Yankee community came to the aid of John Gordon and his brothers and voluntarily defended them at their trials. These good Samaritans were allies of Thomas Wilson Dorr, the great reformer who then languished in prison for his extra-legal effort to improve Rhode Island's government. I believe that the Gordons' most noble advocate was General Thomas F. Carpenter, a distinguished attorney, the unsuccessful reform candidate for governor in 1843 and, later, a convert to Catholicism.

Through subsequent research, I also discovered that the legislators who banned the state's death penalty in 1852 and gave the governor the power to pardon in 1854 were the allies and associates of Thomas Wilson Dorr. Unfortunately, the pardoning power—meant for both Dorr and Gordon—was not invoked because an 1854 revolution in state government brought the nativist Know Nothing Party into power followed soon by the new anti-Irish Republican Party.

My findings concerning the Dorrites and the Irish were published in a 1986 article that won the first-annual writing contest of the *Rhode Island Bar Journal* but did little else. Then in 1993, Charles and Tess Hoffman, professors of English by trade and training, wrote *Brotherly Love: Murder and the Politics of Prejudice in Nineteenth-Century Rhode Island*. With poetic license and subjectivism (coupled with good research), they not only exonerated the Gordons but also implicated U.S. senator William Sprague in the murder of his brother and business partner, Amasa. The Hoffmans were correct in exonerating John Gordon, but their indictment of ambitious Senator William Sprague for conspiracy to commit fratricide is based on very flimsy circumstantial evidence (much like that which convicted John Gordon) and detracts from the credibility of their book.

The final piece of preparatory research for John Gordon's exoneration came in a brief essay by Professor Scott Molloy. He perceptively noted that John Gordon had made his final pre-gallows confession to Father John Brady, who then publicly stated that he had told John to have courage because "you are going to join the noble band of martyrs of your countrymen, who have suffered before at the shine of bigotry and prejudice." This was hardly, says Molloy, an exhortation a priest might give to a confessed murderer; nor was it likely that devout John Gordon, who walked several miles round trip to Sunday Mass, would have withheld his crime from Father Brady while seeking the grace of final repentance.

Unfortunately, dry history cannot compete with dramatic histrionics. By January 2011, noted playwright and Cranston native Kenneth Dooley transformed my research and the insights of Matt Smith, the Hoffmans, Scott Molloy and diocesan historian Reverend Robert Hayman into a spellbinding play entitled *The Murder Trial of John Gordon*, a stage production replete with twenty-three actors. This crisp, moving drama prompted State Representative Peter Martin of Newport to sponsor a resolution seeking justice for John Gordon with a companion resolution then submitted in the Senate by Michael McCaffrey. These initiatives inspired the support of Assistant Public Defender Michael DiLauro, my former student, and the eloquent Father Bernard A. Healey, the governmental liaison for the Diocese of Providence. These advocates rescued the reputation of John Gordon when both houses overwhelmingly approved the Martin-McCaffrey resolutions, and Governor Lincoln Chafee officially pardoned John Gordon on June 29, 2011. This long-delayed pardon made national and international news, as well it should have.

This incredible tale is grippingly and sympathetically related by Rhode Island deputy secretary of state Paul F. Caranci, who occupied a front-row seat for the pardoning process. Embracing the historical dimensions of the office of secretary of state, Paul has become a budding Rhode Island historian with a recent history of his hometown of North Providence also to his credit.

That a writer from a distinguished Italian American family should provide the final word on the trial, the tribulation and the triumph of John Gordon is not completely surprising. Eighty-two years after John Gordon's tragic fate, two young Italian Americans—Nicola Sacco and Bartolomeo Vanzetti—were electrocuted for murder in neighboring Massachusetts. Similarities abound between this inglorious version of blind justice and the Gordon saga. In both, the defendants were recent immigrant arrivals, Catholic in religion (at least nominally), members of the working class and supporters of unpopular political views. In both, the nativist and prejudicial tenor of the times combined with a repressive legal system to elevate circumstantial evidence beyond the realm of reasonable doubt. In both, the alleged perpetrators were denied post-conviction relief or governmental clemency and were executed. In both, sober reflection produced widespread skepticism about actual guilt and led many to question the wisdom of capital punishment. Will John Gordon's pardon, as documented by Caranci, have repercussions in Massachusetts? Only time will tell.

Paul's absorbing book concludes the saga of John Gordon. He has the honor of providing its finishing touch. He has done so not only by drawing on previous research but also by visiting the scenes of the crime and by thoroughly examining the public documents entrusted to his care. His thoughtful, well-crafted, meticulously detailed book is not only a compelling forensic brief for the defense but also a record of John Gordon's final triumph over a legal system once blinded by bigotry and a chief justice (Job Durfee) who epitomized it.

We must keep in mind, warns famed defense attorney Alan Dershowitz, "the limited though important role of the jury in Anglo-American law. Its verdict decides the case before it on the basis of admissible evidence. But it does not decide the historical truth." The conviction of John Gordon is an excellent example of a divergence between the verdict of a misled jury and the verdict of history. Paul Caranci has uncovered the historical truth.

Patrick T. Conley
Historian Laureate of Rhode Island

Section I

THE CONFLUENCE OF EVENTS CREATES AN ATMOSPHERE CONDUCIVE TO AN AMERICAN MISCARRIAGE OF JUSTICE

Chapter 1

ROGER WILLIAMS ORGANIZES A NEW COLONY AND DELIVERS A ROYAL CHARTER WITH EARTH-SHATTERING IMPLICATIONS

Roger Williams's life in the Massachusetts Bay Colony was beginning to unravel. Word had reached him that he was now in danger. He'd been tipped off that exile was imminent, but now he wasn't so sure if the powers that be would settle for mere banishment. Roger Williams was starting to rub the Puritans of Massachusetts the wrong way, and he had reason to believe that he might be sent back to England, where his recent antics would mean certain imprisonment. He no longer had the luxury of time. He would need to leave the colony fast, even before the harsh cruelties of the New England winter could play out in favor of a more travel-conducive spring.

Six years earlier, a more optimistic Williams had boarded the English vessel *Arbella* for the two-month journey that delivered him to the shores of Salem in June 1630. It was the same town that fellow Englishman William Sprague had immigrated to only two years before. Williams's arrival in the New World marked his departure from the corrupt church of Old England where King James tortured Catholics and Protestants alike, depending on his religion of choice at any given time. Puritans were simply dragged out of church and hanged. So much a part of government were the King's religious beliefs that James went so far as to order the printing of his own translation of the Bible, one that preached total compliance to authority. Williams hoped that a new life in America would offer an opportunity to participate in the leadership of a reformed church in New England, where people were free to praise the god of their choice however they chose. In New England, he would be able to "create a true Church of England; one not based on the myopic edicts of a single pope, but rather one more attendant to piety than politics or preferment." Indeed, his impeccable reputation and extraordinary educational background immediately earned him an offer to become the deacon of the Puritan Church of Boston. This prestigious offering was an absolute indication of the high esteem with which the church establishment held this generous and well-versed immigrant. Yet Williams turned down the offer, believing that even the Puritan church in this new land wasn't pure enough to satiate the moral aptitude of his most devout soul. Despite Governor Winthrop's call for a pious city on the hill, Williams's vision was for a slightly different type of city. His English mentor, Sir Edward Coke, arguably the greatest jurist to ever live, taught Williams much. Among his many lessons, Williams learned that a man's home is his "castle," an analogy that likened the peasant to royal status in his most comfortable and safe place. Coke advocated that not even the king is above the law and applied the concept of habeas corpus to the king himself. Indeed, Coke was imprisoned, though eventually released, for his treasonous talk. The death of King James paved the way for Charles I to assume the throne. The new king agreed to Coke's petition of rights, but almost before the ink of the covenant was dry, he violated its terms and decided to dissolve Parliament. The lawmakers, however, were able to pass all their resolutions before the king's guards could break in and arrest them. Roger Williams observed all this and witnessed men being exposed to the cruelties of imprisonment rather than relent their fervor for their principals.

Williams had other influences in his life. While Coke was influential in shaping Williams's thoughts, Sir Francis Bacon, Coke's arch rival, taught Williams how to think. He was able to apply these qualities to the third major influence in his life: Holy Scripture. Williams realized that no one interpretation of the Bible is of greater value than the next. Williams brought all these distinctions with him to the new land.

As the Massachusetts winter of 1636 appeared with a fury, Williams and a small band of Loyalists stepped out into the bitterly cold, snowy night in a state of total apprehension. The barest essentials—food, clothing and shelter—were hard enough to acquire when one was established and had the months of summer to plan for winter's onslaught. How would survival be possible on the run without the necessary preparations? Where would Williams and his followers end up, and what challenges and dangers would meet them there and along the way?

His first three years in the Bay Colony had gone reasonably well. Williams preached under the tutelage of Pastor Ralph Smith and "began a long and

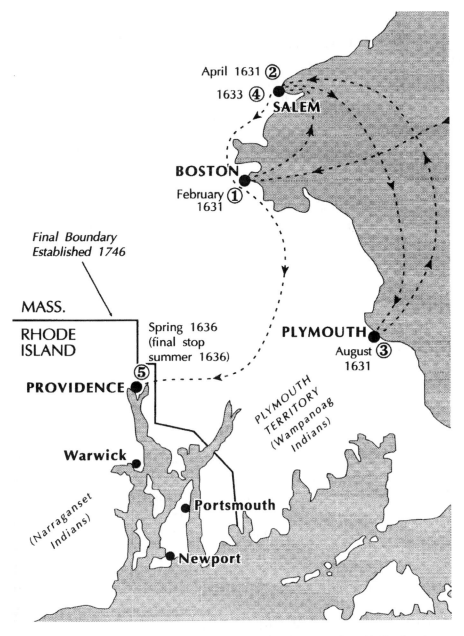

This map shows the routes taken by Roger Williams on his journey from England to the Massachusetts Bay Colony in 1630, during his travels in the Bay Colony, and then on his journey to the Rhode Island Colony following his banishment from Massachusetts in 1636. *Reprinted from* Liberty of Conscience *by Edwin S. Gaustad.*

sensitive relationship with the neighboring Indians. His wife, Mary, blessed him with their first child, and Roger continued to ponder the requirements of true separation." Governor William Bradford of Plymouth found Williams engaging, describing him as "Godly and zealous, having many special parts." Yet as time passed, the governor grew concerned that Williams had perhaps become a bit more zealous than godly, writing in 1633 that he had fallen "into some strange opinions which caused some controversy between the church and him." Williams objected passionately to the "monstrous and most inhumane conversions" forced on the Native Americans on both American continents. He denounced the European practices that he thought he had left behind and went even further, saying that English Americans also deserved better, using his pulpit to advocate the total separation of matters civil and ecclesiastical. He believed that while the state was expected to enforce the provisions of the second tablet of the ten commandments, those dealing with societal issues such as murder, perjury, thievery and the like, it had no business injecting itself into matters of belief such as placing God first in life, observing the Sabbath and other commandments contained within the first tablet.

Williams failed to heed the several warnings of friends, civic and church leaders and the courts. He rejected opportunities to recant and failed to be silent despite the court's initial attempts at leniency. Finally, the Puritan establishment could take no more. When the court reconvened in October 1635, it discussed Williams's heresy, writing, "Whereas Mr. Roger Williams, one of the elders of the church at Salem, hath broached & divulged diverse new & dangerous opinions, and whereas he had questioned and defamed both magisterial and clerical authority, and whereas he maintained his objectionable opinions without hint of repentance or retraction, it is therefore ordered, that the said Mr. Williams shall depart out of this jurisdiction within six weeks." Failure to abide by the order would result in his forceful ejectment. Once again the court had shown Williams leniency, giving him six weeks to get his affairs in order before his banishment. Because his second child had just been born, those six weeks would have served him well. But while Williams refrained from speaking publicly of his beliefs, he continued his discourse with those who visited his home. Within a month, word of Williams's continued disobedience spread to Boston. Williams was summoned back to court but was too ill to attend. In his absence, the court decided that Williams needed to be sent back to England immediately and dispatched a sea captain to Salem to arrest him and carry out the order. Friends within the government tipped him off, however, and when authorities arrived at the Williams home, they found it empty. Williams had fled about three days earlier.

On a bitterly cold January day in 1636, a very ill Roger Williams pressed into the freezing winds of winter and journeyed on foot through the dense snow toward what he hoped would represent a greener pasture. He relied on the guidance and assistance of "savages" from the Wampanoag Indian tribe for fourteen long and torturous weeks, eventually arriving at the headwaters of Narragansett Bay. There he was cordially greeted by the local natives and accepted their spirited invitation to remain in peace. Through agreement with Narragansett Indian Sachems Meauntonomi and Caunaunicus, Williams was allowed to occupy a great deal of land, which was solidified through the granting of the oldest deed in the New World still known to exist. He called his new land Providence and sent for family and friends who shared his beliefs so that they might join him and share in his new home. Williams was determined to establish a "settlement where the civil power should have no authority in spiritual matters and every man could be free to think for himself." He wrote a compact used to govern his new settlement. He ignored the traditional language of the compacts of the period, which all noted that the colony was founded for the glory of God and the advancement of the Christian religion. Williams's language in the compact was, instead, entirely secular. Desiring the complete freedom of the soul, Williams's compact called for soul liberty. His tiny settlement grew steadily with the influx of others who were under the displeasure of the Massachusetts Puritan government. News spread rapidly about this "shelter for persons distressed of conscience" and created fear in the government of Massachusetts that his heresy might spread to the Bay Colony. For the next twenty-seven years, Williams and his followers fostered and strengthened their relationship with the Narragansett Indians and developed new local governments on the Island of Aquidneck and in the Providence Plantations that he established.

These governments served the residents of the colony well, but there were those who craved more. With intensified pressure from Massachusetts, Williams realized that without a new colonial charter granting English recognition to the Colony of Rhode Island and Providence Plantations—one that would provide a foundation for the colony's government and an outline of the broad freedoms that the inhabitants of the colony enjoyed—the colony and its freedoms might be in jeopardy. Consequently, Williams and Dr. John Clarke were dispatched to England as Rhode Island's agents. Williams returned to Rhode Island shortly thereafter, however, leaving Dr. Clarke to draft a new charter representing Williams's desires and present it to England's monarch, King Charles II, which Clarke did in July 1663. The brutal king, who had little tolerance for independent thought in old England, approved the charter, granting broad liberties to his subjects in New England. Clarke sailed for home with the document in hand and delivered it to the colony the following November. There, Captain George Baxter read the charter to the freemen of the Rhode Island Colony on November 24, 1663. The assembly voted to notify the king of their thanks and send a gratuity to Dr. Clarke.

The new governing document contained provisions unheard of in both the New and Old Worlds. The Royal Charter recognized the Native Americans as the rightful owners of the land and required colonists to purchase that land from the Indians. Another unique feature was the extensive protection of the rights of conscience granting religious freedom to inhabitants of the Colony of Rhode Island and Providence Plantations. The protection extended to include not only tolerance of religion but also complete freedom to practice the religion of choice free of government interference. Finally, the new charter offered democratic freedoms to this colony not found in any other. Residents of Rhode Island Colony would be allowed to make their own laws and elect their own leaders within very broad guidelines. This lively experiment defined the authority of executive and legislative branches, designated a number of representatives for each town and created the positions of governor, deputy governor and ten assistants that would initiate the new government.

Yet despite the good intentions of the written words, the notions of religious liberty and the spirit of toleration that were so eloquently and elaborately advocated by Roger Williams and enumerated in Rhode Island's Royal Charter of 1663 stood in marked contrast to the bigotry and religious intolerance that existed in the 1840s. For some reason, the religious liberty that so distinguished the lively experiment was not sustained with the emergence of Irish immigration to Rhode Island.

Chapter 2

THE SPRAGUE FAMILY

An Accumulation of Financial Wealth and Immense Political Power

When Tristram Sprague was born in October 1550, politically motivated arrests and prosecutions by the English Crown over religious differences were still commonplace. The self-serving persecutions made infamous during the reign of King Henry VIII didn't end with his death in 1547. In fact, they continued and, if possible, worsened under the leadership of the successors who vied for his throne of supremacy.

These were the conditions that flourished when twenty-five-year-old Tristram Sprague took Elizabeth Colt of Puddletown as his wife. A year later, the couple gave birth to a son, Edward. The Spragues were fullers by trade, an ancient craft that is an essential part of finishing newly woven cloth. The seemingly endless supply of fleece from the sheep and cattle that thrived in the lush, rolling green landscape of meadows and tillage that graced the countryside of the county of Dorset in Upwey, England, allowed the family business to flourish. Despite their wealth and prosperity in the small seaport hamlet, Tristram and his wife witnessed the brutality of the persecutions and wanted better for their son.

When Edward grew to adulthood, he married Christian Holland, and the two moved into a Dorchester mill house near the River Wey, a small stream that worked the mill for fulling. From accounts, it appears that Edward died in 1614 at the age of forty, leaving behind his wife and six children all under the age of twenty-one. With their father now gone, three of his sons—Ralph, Richard and nineteen-year-old William—chose to journey to America in the interests of the Massachusetts Bay Company, each paying his own transportation. The three, along with Governor John Endecott, boarded the *Abigail* in early July 1628 for the treacherous journey to America.

The group arrived on the shores of Naumkeag (Salem), Massachusetts, three months later on September 6, 1628, and settled in Charlestown. According to Thomas Prince's *Chronology*, all three, and a few others, were employed by Governor Endicot to explore and take possession of the country westward. They traveled through the woods to Charlestown on a neck of land called Michawum, between the Mystic and Charles Rivers, where they wintered in small tents and huts. In the spring of 1629, the band laid out the town of Charlestown. On February 10, 1634, the order creating a board of selectmen was passed and signed by Captain Richard and William Sprague. Governor John Winthrop praised their efforts in orations, saying: "They are the founders of the settlement in this place, and were persons of character, substance and enterprise; excellent citizens, generous public benefactors, and the heads of a very large and respectable family of descendants."

William met Millicent Eames of Hingham, a town about eighteen miles distant, and fell in love. He married her in about 1634 or 1635 and made their home in Hingham, Massachusetts, where her father granted them land on Union Street. William continued to purchase significant amounts of land and became a prominent citizen of his new town, becoming a selectman in 1645 and the town's constable and collector of town rates in 1662. The couple had a total of ten children, among them a son, William, born on May 7, 1650.

Young William learned farming and tilling while living with his family in Hingham. By the time he married his second wife, Mary Tower, he had learned much more. The couple raised at least six children, and in about 1710, when William was in his early sixties, he and Mary moved to Providence, Rhode Island, where William lived out the final years of his life owning and working an extensive and successful farming enterprise. On his death in 1723, William divided his estate among his children, who included Peter Sprague, a son conceived in William's old age.

Peter had been born on October 1, 1714, in the city of Providence. He was just nine years old when his father died yet was left half of his father's homestead in Cranston. On January 10, 1745, Peter purchased the other half of the homestead from his brother Rowland for £800, thereby owning the entire property. He married a woman named Hannah, and the couple had a son, William, and a daughter, Amy. The family continued to live in Cranston, where Peter eventually died on May 4, 1790, naming his son the

An early twentieth-century postcard of the Sprague mansion, circa 1908, at 1351 Cranston Street built by William Sprague II in the 1790s. The addition was added in 1863 by Amasa Sprague II. This home was the birthplace of two Rhode Island governors (William Sprague III and William Sprague IV) and the residence of Amasa Sprague and his family at the time of his murder on December 31, 1843. *From the collection of Robert Wilkins*

1839 portrait of Amasa Sprague. *From* Brotherly Love *by Charles and Tess Hoffmann.*

executor of his estate, located about three and a half miles southwest of Weybosset Bridge over the Pocasset River.

Peter's son, William, farmed the land he acquired and took advantage of the running Pocasset River to build and operate both a sawmill and a gristmill on the property, the same spot that would later house the A&W Sprague Mill on Cranston Street. He also owned a large tract of woodland in the western part of the town of Cranston. William married Isabella Waterman on December 22, 1765, and had several children, including Abner (1767), Sarah (1769), William II (June 5, 1773) and Peter. William's will indicates that he left a wife without children, suggesting that Isabella had died and he had remarried before his death on April 1, 1795.

Like his brothers, William Sprague II was a Cranston farmer. At five feet ten inches tall, William had brown hair and eyes and a light complexion. He was a stout man, weighing nearly two hundred pounds. He was easy in manner but tough in speech and had a very pleasant expression though he was seldom seen to smile. A few months after the settlement of his father's estate, he married Anna Potter, the daughter of a farmer and a woman ten years his senior. Anna was of great assistance to William in the accumulation of property and tended to all the responsibilities of both the house and the five children. It was probably this William, and not his father, who built the home at 1351 Cranston Street, known as the Sprague mansion, sometime around 1790. Largely because of Anna, William was free to tend to his business enterprises, which were many. While not a very sharp dresser, William was an extremely hard worker and one not afraid to soil his clothes. At various points in his life, William engaged in cattle-raising, log cutting, banking, store ownership and management and mill operation, having inherited his father's sawmill and gristmill. In 1808, he converted the gristmill on the banks of the Pocasset River into a small cotton mill where cotton was spun and carded, making William one of the earliest manufacturers of cotton cloth in Rhode Island.

In 1813, Sprague's wooden mill burned to the ground. Arson was suspected, and a man was in fact arrested; but the necessary proof to bring an indictment was lacking. Though he received many offers of assistance, William relied on no one but his two sons Amasa and William III, the oldest males of his five children, to rebuild his mill. The new mill, constructed with stone and masonry, expanded the size and operation adding new and improved machinery, including water-driven power looms that allowed for decreased production costs and increased output. That modernization was due in large part to the enterprise of young William, who convinced his

The Sprague Mill after the expansion by William Sprague following the death of his brother. *Photo by the author, 2012.*

father that he would be able to succeed in implementing a technology at which so many others had failed.

By this time the Sprague enterprises were a true family venture. William's daughter Susanna, the oldest of the five children, and her husband, Baldish Mathewson, were dispatched to Baltimore to establish a commission house where William could sell his goods. Amasa was sent to Groton, Connecticut, to open a store where he could put out his cotton yarn to be woven for the families of the neighborhood. Amasa was the oldest son, and his father relied on him extensively. He had limited formal education but great strength of mind and business talent. His 190-pound body on his five-foot-nine-inch frame gave him a robust appearance. His dark hair and light complexion gave him a certain appeal to women, and his affable nature made him well liked among others. Like his father, he cared little about his dress and never cared much to mingle with those of a haughty demeanor. It was in Groton that Amasa became acquainted with Fanny Morgan, a shoemaker's daughter and a woman whom he would take for his wife in 1822.

William called on Amasa to return to Cranston, however, to superintend the cotton mill and other works going on there. It was clear that Amasa was

This circa-1950s photo is of one of the houses built for the managers of the Sprague Mill. It is located at the corner of Cranston Street and Howard Street. *Photo from* Cranston *by Lydia L. Rapoza and Bette Miller.*

Spraguesville included boardinghouses built in the 1860s for unmarried millworkers. Such structures were part of the expansion of the mill and village that William Sprague ordered following the death of his brother. *Photo from* Cranston *by Lydia L. Rapoza and Bette Miller.*

an integral part of his father's print works operation, which by 1824, had grown to include bleaching cloth and printing calico in Cranston.

Shortly after Amasa was called back home to attend to his father's increasing business needs, Susanna's twenty-nine-year-old husband died unexpectedly. William II left immediately for Baltimore to accompany his daughter and her four children back home to Cranston. Although remarrying shortly after her return, Susanna herself would die a short time later at the age of twenty-seven.

The Spragues were by this time extraordinarily wealthy and popular both socially and politically, having friends in very high places. William II continued to expand his empire with the 1826 purchase of half of the waterpower at Natick Falls, in Kent County, Rhode Island. Industrialists William and Christopher Rhodes purchased the other half. Together they built an extremely large mill complex and village, the oversight of which was entrusted to the care of William Sprague III.

William II was relatively moderate politically, being generally satisfied with any good man elected to represent the town or hold any state office. That changed with the New York abduction of William Morgan, allegedly at the hands of the Free Masons. The event transformed William II into a radical, almost violent anti-Mason, and he did all he could to overthrow the order in Rhode Island. In 1832, he actually became a candidate for governor on the Anti–Free Mason ticket. Both Republican James Fenner and incumbent Lemuel Arnold soundly beat him. Rhode Island did not adopt a plurality provision until 1893, and because no candidate received a majority vote, Arnold remained the governor.

By 1833, in addition to the other interests in their empire, the Spragues controlled three banks and were looking to add another to their dominion. But age, hard work and the bitterness of political losses were beginning to take their toll on William II. Not satisfied with his fortunes, he bitterly opposed the members of the legislature who voted for a tax on banks and worked hard to defeat them during their reelection efforts. Now, the entire Sprague family was united in their hatred of the Masonry, and they became consumed with the notion of defeating anyone of that political persuasion. William III won a seat in the state legislature from Warwick in 1829 and worked on the House Committee to Investigate the Charges Against Masonic Lodges in the State. His work earned him a sterling reputation and helped him win election as Speaker of the House in 1833. From that position he continued to successfully promote the passage of anti-Masonic legislation. Amasa, too, was elected to the state legislature in 1832, 1840 and 1841.

The Sprague Meeting House was built in 1825 and served as a place of worship for many non-Catholic residents of Spraguesville. The belfry was added in 1864 when the building was moved to its present location. *Photo from* Cranston *by Lydia L. Rapoza and Bette Miller.*

While Amasa was more focused on his business interest, William III's political ascendancy was just taking hold. He won a seat in the U.S. Congress on March 4, 1836, and it looked like nothing might interfere with the Sprague ambition until one mid-March morning in 1836. While sitting down to breakfast, William II managed to get a piece of spare rib bone lodged in his throat. He harnessed his own horse and rode three and a half miles into Providence for surgical aid. The doctor advised him to return home where he would come and attend to him. Despite the doctor's advice that the bone should be surgically removed at his home, Sprague objected, instead insisting that it be forced down into his stomach. The surgeon reluctantly complied but, in the process, caused an inflammation of the throat that led to William's death on March 28, 1836.

While William II left ample holdings to his youngest son, Benoni, and daughter, Almira, the vast part of his estate was left to his older sons, Amasa and William III, on whom he had relied to help build his empire. Their father's death dealt a temporary blow to the oldest Sprague brothers' political power in Rhode Island, but they were soon able to recoup. Wealthy and powerful beyond imagination, the two brothers now had sole ownership of the A&W Sprague Mill and its other enterprises. Yet they

Circa 1963 aerial view of Spraguesville shows the mansion, the print works, several mill houses and land on which the Spragues' farm was located at the time of Amasa's murder. *Courtesy of the Rhode Island Division of Statewide Planning.*

William Sprague's expansion plans also included the construction of the White Village, new houses meant for additional workers hired for the extended mill. *Photo by the author, 2012.*

These mill houses on Dyer Avenue are in the original mill village area. *Photo by the author, 2012.*

couldn't agree on how best to manage the empire. William was desirous of an expanded mill operation but too occupied with political matters to take care of it himself. Amasa, on the other hand, to whom the responsibility of overseeing the mill's daily operation fell, seemed content to continue to maintain the status quo. In January 1838, perhaps as a means of keeping closer watch over his brother's handling of their enterprise, William III accepted the Whig nomination for governor of Rhode Island. Though successful, he lost his reelection bid in 1839. In 1840, however, he took a seat in the state legislature and held it until February 5, 1842, when he was elected to the United States Senate. His departure to Washington would make it more difficult to watch over his business affairs, but it also removed him from the political turmoil that was beginning to envelop the state, where so many Irish millworkers were denied participation in their government. Events would soon reach a boiling point.

Chapter 3

IRISH CATHOLIC IMMIGRANTS
ARE BLAMED AND PUNISHED FOR REBELLIOUS
REFORM ATTEMPTS

The 1663 Royal Charter that John Clarke delivered to Rhode Island was such a powerful document that it had survived relatively unchecked for almost 180 years. It provided the sufficient balance of appropriate safeguards and essential liberties necessary to satisfy both the majority of the people and the elected leaders subjected to its rule. However, as the nineteenth century began to unfurl, some began to feel that the Royal Charter needed revision. With Connecticut's adoption of a written constitution in 1818, Rhode Island remained the only state still governed by a royal charter, and "since 1830, when Virginia relented, Rhode Island had been the only state to impose a general real estate requirement for voting and office holding." This stipulation, known as freeman status, began to cause disenfranchisement issues with new immigrants. (Freeman status—or freeholder status, as it was sometimes referred—was a designation granted to male citizens not encumbered by the weight of indebtedness or servitude. Only freemen were allowed to own property, and only property owners were granted the right to vote.)

In 1841, some elected leaders questioned the document's modernity in light of the fact that a new wave of Irish immigrants, who worked the mills, had not yet gained freeholder status. Still more began to advocate for the adoption of a new charter that would address these and other perceived deficiencies of the Royal Charter. Among the other antiquated elements cited by the reformists to support the call for a new constitution was the fact that the charter of 1663 "was unamendable and contained no

Early daguerreotype of Thomas
Wilson Dorr, who led an
unsuccessful rebellion in the
cause of expanded suffrage in
1842. *From the author's collection.*

separation of powers, no bill of rights, and no provision for reapportioning seats in the legislature."

Under this archaic document, the Rhode Island General Assembly was supreme, and that body was "dominated by conservative, landholding white males who saw no need to share their power with those less favorably suited." An earlier, less intense reform effort in 1817 ended with a call for a constitutional convention, but the freemen of the state rejected it. A second reform movement led to a constitutional convention in 1824, but it produced no change. A third movement, this one led by Providence attorney Thomas Wilson Dorr, resulted in another meaningless convention in 1834, which ended, as did the entire movement, after the economic depression of 1837. No reforms were enacted.

New hope was instilled into the reform effort, however, in 1840 when a new movement began emulating the unique and successful political techniques employed by William Henry Harrison and John Tyler in their successful national campaign for president and vice president. A rejuvenated and perhaps less naïve Thomas Dorr and his loyalists resurrected their reform cause. By this time, however, Dorr and others were beginning to believe that their desired reforms would only become reality through government revolution and not by promises of another meaningless constitutional convention.

Although the reform movement was technically non-partisan in nature, most of Dorr's supporters were members of the Democratic Party. They were primarily non-freemen who "advocated universal manhood suffrage and denounced real and personal property qualifications for voting on political (but not financial) questions." Most importantly, the Dorrites, as they became known, were willing to engage in what was considered by some to be illegal, even treasonous, actions in an effort to eradicate long-standing abuses in government.

Just a year earlier, Samuel Ward King, a surgeon from the town of Johnston, was elected governor. The fifty-four-year-old father of fourteen was a vocal opponent of the expansion of voting rights. In response, liberals organized the Rhode Island Suffrage Association. A number of freemen, including former Representative Thomas Dorr and State Representative Samuel Y. Atwell supported the movement, which quickly spread to municipalities throughout the state. Supporters rolled out two newspaper publications, *New Age* and the *Daily Express*, each dedicated to the principles of expanded suffrage.

It wasn't long before the general assembly felt the pressure and, as in the past, authorized a constitutional convention to address the reformers' concerns. But unlike the previous calls to hold constitutional conventions in 1824 and 1834, the 1841 convention call fooled no one advocating reform. The Dorrites knew from experience that the conservative establishment was not offering a sincere proposal for change. Their instincts proved correct when it was learned that only freemen would be allowed to vote for the selection of delegates.

Association members sprang into action organizing a mass meeting to be held in Providence on April 12, 1841. Despite a cold spring rain, almost three thousand people attended to the ringing of city church bells. Bands played special suffrage songs, and parades marched through the streets. Attendees listened to a series of speeches and passed several resolutions. The reformers believed that in the absence of legitimate reform efforts by the general assembly, they would need to take political matters into their own hands. The reformers decided to call their own constitutional convention. All white males twenty-one years of age and older, regardless of property ownership, would be allowed to vote for the delegates. The election took place in August 1841, and the convention of the "People's Party" was scheduled for Monday, October 4, 1841, a month before the convention called by the general assembly.

As the People's Convention opened, the delegates readied themselves for the task of drafting a new constitution, one that would reflect all the ideals of the movement and at the same time become an effective order of government. The draft included a bill of rights and an equal distribution of powers among the three separate branches of government as had been advocated by the suffragists. It also had a clause allowing for the casting of ballots in secret for the first time in Rhode Island and, naturally, contained the all-important abolition of property ownership requirements that prevented so many, particularly the immigrant population, from participating in the electoral process. However, in an effort to gain wider acceptance, the document created certain offices for tax-paying citizens only and maintained property ownership and residency requirements in matters pertaining to municipal finance. While balancing representation in the general assembly through reapportionment, the People's Charter also fixed the number of representatives town by town on a rough population basis, a provision whose absence from the Royal Charter had spurred the call for change.

Meanwhile, the freemen's or landholders' convention gathered on Monday, November 1, 1841. It too drafted a constitution. In many ways, its constitution reflected the People's Constitution, which had already been widely publicized by the second convention's opening day. It too contained a bill of rights and separation of powers among the three branches of government. It did a better job of addressing the issue of legislative apportionment, using population as the determining factor and setting limits of no less than two and no more than eight representatives per city or town. It removed the freemen status requirement and allowed immigrants to vote after three years of naturalization rather than the one-year requirement that had been in effect. However, the landholder's constitution failed to remove the property ownership requirement for naturalized citizens.

The People's Convention reconvened following an impassioned plea, submitted by the "Colored Citizens of Rhode Island," requesting the suffrage of black citizens. Frederick Douglass visited Providence to speak in favor of the cause, one that Dorr idealistically agreed with. Other convention delegates, however, saw the inclusion of black suffrage as the certain death knell to its passage and rejected the notion. The document remained unchanged, and a three-day vote on the referendum began on December 27, 1841. A total of 13,944 white males cast votes on the question, and a mere 52 cast ballots in opposition. Many freemen viewed the vote as an illegal referendum "staged by a band of outlaws" and refused to take part in the process. Just fewer than 50 percent of the 9,950 freemen actually voted in the election. However, with only 23,142 eligible voters, the affirmative votes constituted a clear and convincing majority. The rub was that the eligible voters in the People's referendum included non–property owning white males who were otherwise still ineligible to cast ballots under current law.

Reveling in victory, the suffragists expected that the current government leaders would quietly step down when their terms expired on the first Tuesday of May 1842. Governor Samuel Ward King wasn't about to go quietly into the good night, however. King took his case to the federal court, where Judge Pitman "condemned the People's Convention as criminal and revolutionary." Supreme Court Justice Job Durfee, who believed that the people owed their allegiance to the state and therefore had no power to make such decisions, went much further, writing: "I therefore say to you, that, in the opinion of this court, such a movement…is a movement which can find no justification in law; that if it be a movement against no law in particular, it is, nevertheless, a movement against the law; that it is not a mere movement for a change of rulers, or for a legal reform in government, but a movement which, if carried to its consequences, will terminate the existence of the state itself." He went on to authorize freemen to vote on their constitution, declaring that if it passed, anyone supporting the People's Constitution in its stead would have committed treason: "Treason against the state—treason perhaps against the United States—for it will be an attempt by the overt act of levying war, to subvert a State which is an integral part of the Union, and to levy war against one state, to that end, we are all apprehensive will amount to levying war against all."

Dorr and eight others, including Samuel Y. Atwell, drafted and signed a counter argument entitled, "The Right of the People to Form a Constitution: The Nine Lawyers' Opinion." This was a clear implication that, like the freemen, the Dorrites were not ready to concede the issue. This clearly set the stage for insurrection.

With the battle lines drawn, the Dorrites readied themselves for the intense struggle ahead. Some of Dorr's supporters were Irish immigrants who owned no land. Many were common laborers without significant skills. Many were uneducated, and most lived on the fringes with little or no wealth to speak of. The freemen, who organized under the banner of the Law and Order Party, made the fight personal and sought to build division between the Irish immigrants and the Yankee establishment, who feared the threat of a future influx of Irish immigrants: "In an era when 'foreigner' was largely synonymous with 'Irish,' many whispered of dark Catholic plots, and Help Wanted ads included the phrase, 'No Irish Need Apply.'" As was typical of the mid-nineteenth century, broadsides were widely used by both factions to deliver "campaign" messages. The Law and Order Party, however, effectively utilized broadsides to warn that approving the People's Constitution would "place your government, your civil and political institutions, your PUBLIC SCHOOLS, and perhaps your RELIGIOUS PRIVILEGES under the control of the POPE OF ROME, through the medium of thousands of NATURALIZED FOREIGN CATHOLICS." The same broadside accused Irish immigrants of violently breaking into a peaceful assembly of American citizens in New York City and forcibly disrupting proceedings. It described the Irish as "bands of filthy wretches…drunken loafers; scoundrels who the police and criminal courts would be ashamed to receive in their walls, course [*sic*] blustering rowdies; bleary eyed and bloated offscourgings from the stews, blind alleys, and real lanes; disgusting objects bearing the form human, but who the sow in the mire might almost object to as companions." The slanderous broadside even described the Catholic priests as "sly deceitful villains" who encouraged such mob tactics. The implication was clear that if the People's Constitution were to pass, Rhode Islanders could expect the same disgusting behavior here at home. Scare tactics included threats that St. Patrick would replace the iconic Roger Williams just as the shamrock would replace the anchor as the state symbol and "hope" as its motto. The sides were clearly drawn, and even Dorr's Yankee family, with whom he still lived, opposed the suffrage for which Thomas was about to risk his life.

Amid the scare tactics and degradations of the Irish immigrants, people were cast into such division that not even the freemen's constitution could garner the support sufficient to pass. Many people were confused and frightened, not knowing what to expect if the Irish were allowed to take control of the government. Against this backdrop, and threatened with a charge of treason, Dorr and his suffragists prepared to hold their own elections under the People's Constitution. Anticipating the worst political situation imaginable, the government led by Samuel Ward King responded immediately with a legislative act authorizing a new law, dubbed the Algerine law, that deemed any meeting and election held under the People's Constitution illegal and void while making any person running for office under this constitution guilty of a high crime and misdemeanor. Furthermore, the law charged that anyone elected and attempting to hold office under the People's Constitution would be guilty of treason and sentenced to life in prison. The law specifically designated the Rhode Island Supreme Court as the judicial body charged with enforcement of the act. This was not coincidental as it was widely believed that because the supreme court was a body conveniently handpicked by the general assembly, it would likely rule interpretations in the assembly's favor. By this point, the broadside

NATIVE AMERICAN CITIZENS!

READ AND TAKE WARNING!

A SHORT SERMON.

LET EVERY SOUL BE SUBJECT TO THE HIGHER POWERS. *Romans*, 13, 1.

Christians, like all other men, have the right to protect themselves against oppression. They have also the right to aid in the protection of others, but our Savior said, "MY KINGDOM IS NOT OF THIS WORLD," and thus taught his followers that it was inconsistent with their duty to him, and with their respect for his doctrines, to mingle in the strife for power. Paul, in the above quoted text, did not intend to teach his brethren that they should submit, with degrading servility, to tyranny, cruelty, and oppression, when they could remove the evil without producing another equally great. But his frequent exhortations, as well as those of his DIVINE MASTER, fully show that they considered it the indispensable duty of CHRISTIANS to submit to existing governments for the sake of peace, until oppression became too cruel to be borne, or until the evil could be remedied without unnecessary violence; and that, in ALL CASES, for the HONOR of the CHURCH, the SUCCESS of the GOSPEL, and the PEACE of the COMMUNITY, CHRISTIANS should "be subject to the HIGHER POWERS," as *long as forbearance would be a virtue*.

CHRISTIAN PROFESSORS OF RHODE ISLAND, I put to you a plain question.—Will you answer it as on the ALTAR of GOD, to HIM AND YOUR OWN CONSCIENCES? Does it appear that the Constitution is to be voted on for adoption or rejection, on the 21st, 22d, and 23d, inst. is of such a character as to threaten danger to your rights and privileges, or those of others? Is it oppressive in its provisions or bearings? Would you be justified in rejecting it, and in adopting another which will place your government, your civil and political institutions, your PUBLIC SCHOOLS, and perhaps your RELIGIOUS PRIVILEGES, under the control of the POPE of ROME, through the medium of THOUSANDS of NATURALIZED FOREIGN CATHOLICS? Does the honor and prosperity of the church require it? Do the peace, welfare, and prosperity, of the State require it? Yet, reject the Constitution now presented to you, and you show your preference for another, which, *should it ever be adopted*, WILL PLACE THE BALLANCE OF POWER IN THE STATE, IN THE HANDS OF THOSE PEOPLE. The event can readily be predicted: Would you defend yourselves and your church against the operations and predominance of such a power, and preserve the State

from anarchy and ruin? Would you preserve peace, and thereby avoid violence and bloodshed? Would you pay that respect to the CONSTITUTED AUTHORITIES WHICH THE GOSPEL DEMANDS? Would you keep a conscience pure and undefiled, by pursuing a course on which you can hereafter look with approbation, and for the correctness of which, you can CONFIDENTLY APPEAL TO HEAVEN IN THE HOUR OF DEATH, AND AT THE DREAD TRIBUNAL HEREAFTER? Then, and I must suppose such to be your wish, array yourselves on the side of the "HIGHER POWERS," in a quiet and peaceable manner, GIVE YOUR VOTES FOR THE CONSTITUTION ON MONDAY NEXT. Show those who act in the opposition only to carry out their will, that you value too highly your CHRISTIAN PROFESSION, your CHRISTIAN CHARACTER, and your CHRISTIAN PRINCIPLE, to countenance sedition, and to endanger the peace of an entire community, only to defeat the benevolent object of the existing government, and to give encouragement and support to a spirit of violence and disorder. Tell those who would allure you to aid them in the work of strife. WE HAVE NOT SO LEARNED CHRIST.

REV. WILLIAM S. BALCH.

The above gentleman, late Pastor of the First Universalist Church in this city, and who, while here, did much for the party which have made and voted for the "People's Constitution," was requested by him and others to lecture during his visit here this week from New York. He very properly refused to do so; and said he would not care he now a resident here; for the reason, that the party have carried the thing too far, and are now making a political affair of it, and he would have nothing to do with it. This is valuable testimony from one of the ablest and fastest friends of the suffrage cause.

AN EXAMPLE.

In a "Short Sermon" published in our extra sheet, the writer alluded to the possibility that, should a constitution like that called the "People's Constitution" be adopted, the naturalized foreign Catholics might exercise a pernicious influence on our political, civil, and religious institutions, and on our public schools. We have a case in point. The CATHOLIC BISHOP HUGHES, of New York, at the last election in that city, ARRAYED UNDER HIS CONTROL, some THREE THOUSAND FOREIGN CATHOLIC voters, after an effort of a few days, to sustain at the BALLOT BOX his own views on the question of public schools, for the purpose of diverting to the use of the CATHOLIC CHURCH, a portion of the common school fund of the State. With a

longer period for the purpose, it is probable a body of foreign naturalized Catholics might have been organized, and will hereafter be organized, in that city and State, under PAPAL ECCLESIASTICAL INFLUENCE, to carry out their views. The excitement on the question still continues. The Bishop and his party are determined to succeed in their efforts. The native citizens have become alarmed. And meetings have been held to prevent the abhorred attempt from becoming successful.

On Wednesday last, a meeting was held in the Park, New York city, on the question. And during the proceedings, a band of foreigners broke in upon the assemblage, and by means of violence broke up the meeting. A New York paper says— "Our cheeks are suffused with shame and indignation as we publish this matter; for so gross an insult to our rights as Americans, we have never seen or heard of before. Bands of filthy wretches, whose every touch was offensive to a decent man, drunken loafers; scoundrels who the police and criminal courts would be ashamed to receive in their walls; coarse, blustering rowdies, blear eyed and bloated offscourings from the stews blind alleys and rear lanes; disgusting objects bearing the form human, but whom the sow in the mire might almost object to as companions—these were they who broke into the midst of a peaceful body of American citizens—struck and insulted the chosen officers of the assemblage, and with shrieks, loud blasphemy, and howling in their hideous native tongue, prevented the continuance of the customary routine. We saw Irish priests there—sly, false, deceitful villains—looking on and evident encouraging the gang who created the tumult. We noticed two or three tavern bullies strike on the head a presiding officer—one of the most aged and respectable men of our city. We beheld the whole body of those officers forced at length, from their seats, and driven, with jibe and blows, from the stage. And these officers were native Americans—men with grey heads—men known for long years among us, as gentle men of reputation, philanthropy and exalted worth— And is New York to utter no loud voice of abhorrence towards this transaction? Is this hypocritical scoundrel Hughes, and his minions, to drill ranks of ignorant and vindictive followers—and send them forth to act as these wretches acted—and shall no note be taken of it? It is a blot and an insolent violation of our dearest and most glorious privileges. The whole city—the whole state—ought to rise up as one man, and let these jesuitical knaves, and their apt satellites, know what it is to feel the blast from an injured and outraged country."

RHODE-ISLANDERS—Read this. Ponder seriously on it. Say—are you prepared to witness such scenes enacted in your little, and hitherto peaceful and prosperous State? Are you prepared to see a Catholic Bishop, at the head of a posse of Catholic Priests, and a band of their servile dependents, take the field to subvert your institutions, under the sanction of a State Constitution. If not, vote for the Constitution now presented to you, which is well calculated to protect you from such abuses. ROGER WILLIAMS.

Those on both sides of the Dorr Rebellion issued broadsides, such as the 1882 example shown here, to promote the interests of their respective causes. *Reprinted from* The Dorr Rebellion: A Study in American Radicalism 1833–1849.

propaganda was so effective that there was a basic fear that the People's Constitution would in fact "bring the state under the domination of the idle, ignorant, and poorer class. They alarmed farmers by contending that the document's reapportionment plan would place agrarian interest at the mercy of the industrial and shift the basis of taxation from business to land; and they excited entrepreneurs by emphasizing the reformer's anticorporate philosophy of equal rights." Lawmakers were convinced that the inclusion of Irish immigrants into the political fray would eventually lead to the "political ascendancy of those Irish-Catholic immigrants who were swarming into the state in ever-increasing numbers."

The sitting government was so aggressive in its attack on the People's Party that the Dorrites were finding it difficult to get candidates to run under its banner, and many supporters ran for cover. The Algerine law was certainly achieving the objective of crushing Dorr's movement. Both sides appealed to the federal government for help, but fifty-two-year-old President John Tyler flatly refused to be the arbiter of the suffrage issue in Rhode Island, pretty much appeasing each side without making any commitment for action.

This was the political landscape on April 18, 1842, when the People's Party held its first election. Thomas Dorr, having failed to convince anyone else to run for governor under the party's banner, was unanimously elected to that post with 6,359 votes and, in the process, alienated many members of his own family. Dorr's election also included a slate of legislators who were elected that same day.

On April 20, just two days later, a second election was held. In this contest, Governor Samuel Ward King garnered 4,864 votes in defeating challenger Thomas Carpenter in a two-to-one landslide. This election, too, included seats in the general assembly. Rhode Island, the smallest state in the Union, now had two governors and two legislatures, one in Providence and the other in Newport.

A crowd estimated at two thousand gathered at Hoyle's Tavern in the West End of Providence on May 3, 1842, to accompany Thomas Wilson Dorr to the Benefit Street statehouse to watch Dorr take his oath as the rightful governor of Rhode Island and his legislature convene in its first session. Two uniformed and armed militia units and marching bands paraded through the streets to the cheering of Dorrite loyalists. However, when the throngs arrived at their destination, they found the doors locked. Hundreds now stood outside the inaccessible statehouse as a light rain began to fall, perhaps foreshadowing things to come. Dorr toyed with the idea of breaking the doors down, but he was out voted, as none were willing to go to such an extreme at that point. Rather, Dorr and the People's Legislature simply moved to the foundry building, an unfinished construction, and convened the first session of government under the People's Legislature with the swearing in of sixty-six legislators and Governor Dorr. Immediately following Dorr's inaugural address, the legislature repealed the Algerine law, which Dorr and his followers viewed as created by a previous, not a rival, legislature.

Portrait of Governor Samuel Ward King (1840–1843), the Johnston physician who was serving as governor during the Dorr Rebellion and at the time of the murder of Amasa Sprague. *Rhode Island State House Portrait Collection.*

Meanwhile, Governor King and his legislators were being sworn in at the Newport statehouse, one of five being used on a rotating schedule until the Smith Hill statehouse was completed in 1901. By now, President Tyler, seemingly in violation of the pledge of neutrality, had dispatched 183 troops from other states to help fortify Fort Adams in Newport in support of the charter government. The very next day, the Law and Order Party began using the Algerine law to arrest members of the People's Party. Among them were Welcome B. Sayles, the People's speaker of the house, and Daniel Brown, a People's representative from Newport. Eventually Dorrites Burrington Anthony, Dutee Pearce and many others would join them in the state prison but not before a final act of defiance. The hostilities had clearly begun as a number of Dorr's loyalists were fired from their jobs and some anti-Dorrites' barns burned. Many Dorrites couldn't take the heat and resigned their seats while others simply walked away. Both sides prepared for a bloody revolution, and each side warned the public, through broadsides and speeches, that the inevitable was about to take place.

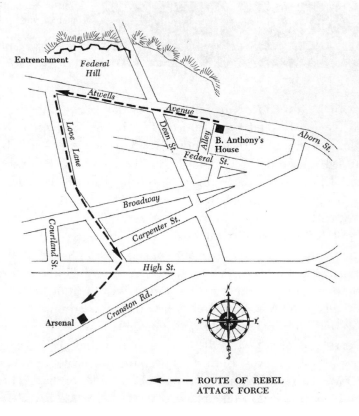

ROUTE OF REBEL
ATTACK FORCE

Above: Depiction of the Dorrite attempt to take control of the arsenal in Providence on May 18, 1842. Dorr's small band of followers fled when their Revolutionary War cannon failed to fire. *Reprinted from* The Dorr Rebellion: A Study in American Radicalism 1833–1849.

Opposite, top: Governor King lived in opulence in this home on the south side of Plainfield Street in the Olneyville section of Johnston. *Reprinted from* Johnston Volume II *by the Johnston Historical Society.*

Opposite, bottom: This map shows the route taken by Dorr and his followers to the Providence arsenal for the ill-fated attack in the early morning hours of May 18, 1842. *From the author's collection.*

Indeed something did. With an arrest warrant hanging over his head, Dorr gathered his supporters in front of the home of Sheriff Burrington Anthony, a loyal supporter who offered his residence on Atwells Avenue as both a shelter and a headquarters. Stepping up onto a carriage, Dorr delivered a forty-five-minute speech in which he claimed to have five thousand men in New York at the ready to attend his cause. He waved a sword he had been given while in New York and noted that "the sword had been bloodied in the name of liberty once before, and he would not hesitate to bloody it again if needed." Once the crowd dispersed, Dorr, Anthony and several others retreated to the comfort of the house to "convene a council of war."

Several of Dorr's supporters in the legislature had taken advantage of the offer of amnesty extended by Governor King, which required takers to denounce the People's Constitution and swear allegiance to the Law and

Order government. Those still loyal to the cause, however, were now more willing to resort to more violent means of maintaining their government. In perhaps one of the poorest kept military secrets, Dorr organized his supporters to take up arms and forcibly overtake the state's arsenal on the Dexter Training Grounds. With two six-pound Revolutionary War cannons obtained from the United Train Artillery Company on College Hill, Dorr advised his supporters to prepare for battle. Governor King did the same. At 1:30 on the morning of May 18, Dorr and about three hundred of his loyalists began the quarter-mile walk through the residential streets of Providence to the armory. Once there, Dorr asked for the defenders' surrender and shortly thereafter ordered his men to fire the cannons. We will never know whether it was the dampness of the night, the age of the cannons, sabotage or simply Divine Providence that caused both cannons to fail; but for that inaction, there may have been a great deal of bloodshed and a significant loss of life. As it was, Dorr's men ran in retreat well before sunrise without a single shot being fired.

Later that morning, Governor King's troops arrived at the Anthony home with an arrest warrant and an offer of a $1,000 reward for Dorr's capture. But, out of concern for his safety, Dorr had long since fled town on his way to the security of another state.

Scene depicting the capture of Acote's Hill in Chepachet that virtually ended the Dorr Rebellion. *From H. Lord print called "Prisoners of War."*

Dorr did eventually return in the summer of 1842 in a final attempt to rally his supporters in Chepachet, not to engage in violence, but rather to convene the People's Legislature; but when word arrived that Governor King had overwhelming forces marching into town, Dorr discharged his followers of less than three hundred loyalists. Once again, a downtrodden Dorr was forced to leave the state for the safer confines of Connecticut and then New Hampshire. Many of Dorr's supporters were rounded up and arrested under the Algerine law, and Governor King raised the reward for Dorr's capture to $5,000.

As the search for Dorr continued, the Irishmen who supported his cause were no better off as a result of the conflict. They were still denied the vote, and many of the old Yankees blamed them for the insurrection perpetrated by Dorr. After spending time in Massachusetts, Connecticut and New Hampshire, Dorr returned to Rhode Island on October 31, 1843, and was promptly arrested by Deputy Sheriff Jabez J. Potter while walking on a street in downtown Providence. He was held at the state prison where many of his supporters still languished. Eventually, he would share the prison with another high-profile person: an Irishman and Cranstonian by the name of John Gordon.

Chapter 4

ONE IRISH CATHOLIC FAMILY'S QUEST FOR OPPORTUNITY

By the 1830s, the mill industry in Rhode Island employed some 3,500 workers. Farmers, no longer able to provide for their families by traditional means, began to seek mill employment, as did many of their family members. Consequently, many of the mill employees were women and children between the ages of six and twelve. The workday was long and the pay minimal. While a skilled adult male could earn as much as nine dollars a week, women were paid only two dollars and children only twenty-five cents for a fourteen-to sixteen-hour workday. Worse, many mill owners paid their employees in scrip that was good only in the mill stores and for rent owed to the mill owner for housing. Frequently, pay was issued monthly, and the entire amount was consumed by credits advanced during the month at the mill store.

Despite the hard work and low wages, overall conditions in America still seemed more attractive than the living conditions of those born across the ocean. During the first quarter of the nineteenth century, Ireland was in political turmoil. A rebellion by the United Irishmen broke out, confirming that Ireland could no longer be governed as a British colony. Economic depression came on the heels of two British foreign wars, the Napoleonic Wars with France and the War of 1812 with the United States. Famine was common, and the government passed the Coercion Acts in an effort to deal more absolutely with suspects as well as criminals, all tending to increase the peasant's misery. The promise of a brighter future in America sparked a new wave of Irish immigration to the United States. In Rhode Island, the foreign population increased from just thirty-nine in the 1820 census to over five thousand by 1842. The Irish Catholics immigrating to Rhode Island settled first in Portsmouth-Newport, Pawtucket and then in Cranston on the west side of the Providence River, clustered around two Catholic churches. Here, their economic welfare depended in large part on the prosperity of the print works owned and operated by the Sprague family. Even those not directly employed by the mill, such as the farmers, tavern keepers and merchants, depended on the patronage of the millworkers for success.

In 1836, the mill village of Spraguesville had a population of over five hundred people, all of whom were almost entirely dependent on the Spragues—who owned the mill, the tenements and the mill store—for employment, housing and provisions. One might argue that they also owned the local politicians. The Spragues' political strength was an extension of their economic power, and the town council members were beholden to them by reason of party politics or economic dependence. The Spragues knew how to use the government system to their advantage at election time. Frequently they would deed small portions of their land to millworkers by quitclaim. Those workers would then qualify for the vote under the property ownership standard. The employee ballots were cast under the watchful eye of the boss for quality assurance purposes, and after the balloting, the property would be quitclaim deeded back to the Spragues. At a time when very small numbers decided elections, such gluts of carefully cast ballots were enough to sway any election.

Despite the local political situation, jobs were plentiful, food was available and opportunities flourished. Such was the allure that induced a determined Nicholas Gordon to leave his family in Ireland for the promise of a new life in America. He arrived in Boston in 1836 but swiftly advanced to Cranston, where he most likely had friends from the old country. He filed a declaration for citizenship in 1837 at Lowell, Massachusetts. Gordon was "a man of much talk; a sportive, swearing little Irishman," according to those who knew him. On short order, he was able to raise or borrow enough money to set up a small business. He was the smartest and most enterprising of his brothers. His little store was located in rented quarters in Knightsville. The Cranston village of Knightsville was about a quarter mile from the print works and inhabited by a high concentration of Irish immigrants, prompting many of the old Yankees to refer to it as Monkeytown. After a very short time, Gordon moved to Spraguesville and opened a general store there, also in rented quarters. Conducting business in this part of town presented a much better opportunity for him because he was able to take advantage

The mill houses in Spraguesville circa 1950. *Courtesy of the Rhode Island State Archives.*

Turn-of-the-century photograph of Spraguesville at the corner of Cranston Street and Dyer Avenue showing the print works and several mill houses. *Photo from* Cranston *by Lydia L. Rapoza and Bette Miller.*

of the patronage of the millworkers who could conveniently visit his store before or after work. The store was strategically located on Cranston Street just around the corner to the west of the mill and on the opposite side of the street. Here Gordon sold groceries, candy and notions such as thread, needles, pins and tape. Because the mill store prices were as much as 25 percent higher than the same items sold elsewhere, the millworkers and others realized that "things could be got as cheap of him as of anybody." One such patron was Miss Susan Field. Field was a known prostitute who lived and worked in downtown Providence but would visit Gordon's store every time she was in Cranston, and most weeks, she later insisted, that was as much as three times.

After a few years, Gordon was fully assimilated into the neighborhood, and he knew how the political system worked. Although business was good, he knew that if he could obtain a license from the Cranston town council to sell liquor, his business would become very profitable. In April 1840, he convinced Councilman Jeremiah Carpenter to post a bond for him, pretty much assuring the council's granting of the license. Carpenter had been married to Susanna Sprague Mathewson at the time of her death. He, like the Spragues, was also a Dorrite at this point in time and probably wished the Irishman success in his venture. Sure enough, at the April meeting of the town council, action was taken granting Gordon the right to sell liquor and wine by the bottle, but not by the drink, which would have required a tavern license. No one opposed the petition on the council, nor did anyone from the public speak against it, probably due in part to Carpenter's support, which may have implied the de facto blessing of the Spragues. The result was the same when Gordon applied to the council for the annual renewal of the license in April 1841. Gordon was making quite a good living.

Sometime around September 1841, Nicholas began to board with Abby N. King. The arrangement was mutually beneficial, providing Abby with the few extra dollars that she needed while freeing Gordon's time that he formerly spent cleaning an apartment, laundering his clothes or cooking his meals and allowing him more time to tend to his work in the store. By September, Gordon had prospered enough to buy a $200 parcel of land on which he built a new store with an upstairs apartment. He was by now a naturalized citizen and believed that the promise of America was everything that he had expected it to be and more.

The dawn of spring delivered more good news. At the April meeting of the Cranston town council, a petition was approved granting Gordon a license to keep an "Ale House at his store and to retail therein in any quantity

Saint Bartholomew Church, originally built as the Spraguesville Meeting House, as it appears today. *Photo by the author, 2012.*

(except on Sundays) wines and strong liquors." Obtaining an alehouse license was a major achievement for Gordon because it was much more lucrative than his former license that only allowed him to sell alcohol by the bottle. Finally Gordon could provide the many workers from the Sprague Mill that stopped in his store at lunch and dinnertime the drink they wanted so badly but couldn't get elsewhere. Now, Gordon thought, he would be able to take advantage of those drink sales that workers might try to sneak in before work or for lunch. And with the passage of the license coming with no objections from the public or the mill owners, Gordon had reason to start to believe in his own invincibility.

One afternoon in June 1842, Gordon attended an auction at Tillinghast Almy's store in Providence. Almy routinely held such auctions and often took in consigned items to include in the sales. Gordon was able to purchase items for a relatively low cost and many times could resell those goods in his own store at a profit. Perhaps it was Dorr's armed invasion and the ensuing insurrection that caused Gordon to eye the gun behind the counter on this particular June day. Or maybe it was simply that he was beginning to feel a need for some increased security at his own store. Whatever the reason, Gordon's successful bid enabled him to take home the light rifle complete with bayonet and equipage. Feeling pretty good about snagging such a handsome piece, Gordon proudly left Almy's store clutching his prize. It wasn't the only time that a gun would grab his attention either. A few months later, on the afternoon of October 7, 1842, Gordon would spot a handgun, one that a man named James Francis once owned, and apparently believe it, too, would make a fine addition to the store. He would take that one home as well.

By mid-summer of 1842, Gordon began feeling a little less himself. Illness required that he live with someone who could help tend to his needs, so he moved in with his friend John O'Brien, providing Gordon the time and rest he needed to recover. O'Brien didn't mind nursing his friend back to health and actually enjoyed his company. Besides, Gordon was little trouble and a hard worker. So hard a worker, in fact, that even though not at full strength, he was able to complete the construction on his store and house in a relatively short time.

For his part, Amasa Sprague had just been elected to the general assembly, where he would join his brother and help the family with their cause of defeating Free Masonry. While Amasa Sprague and Nicholas Gordon were having a great August, things were not so rosy for Thomas Dorr. He had just been indicted for treason under the Algerine law, and Irish Catholics began to feel the pressure of being assigned blame for Dorr's failed insurrection.

Gordon's good fortune followed him into 1843. On April 3, the town council granted a three-month extension of the liquor license. The short-term renewal was not at all indicative of a problem with Gordon's license but rather was reflective of a new mandate from the general assembly. With no problems on his horizon, Gordon decided that it was time to send word back to Ireland that the rest of his family should join him in America. Excited beyond words and very anxious to once again see the family he left behind so many years ago, Gordon penned a letter to his mother, Ellen, noting that he would pay passage for her, his brothers—John, Robert and William—his sister Margaret and William's seven-year-old daughter. William's wife and Ellen's husband, Samuel, had long since passed. After mailing the letter, Gordon made arrangements through the Joseph Murray Company of New York to bring his family to America. Jeremiah Bagot, the company's agent in Providence, was very gracious when they spoke, assuring Gordon that he would tend to everything and leave nothing to chance. Gordon's dream of a better life in America had taken shape, and now he could hardly wait for his family to share in his good fortune.

Gordon realized that, on their arrival, he would need to help his family members get on their feet. He could point them in the right direction as far as employment. In fact, he had a need for an assistant right in his own store. Lodging, on the other hand, would be a more difficult decision. They could rent, he thought, but why not take the opportunity to expand his house and have them stay with him, even if only on a temporary basis? Business was booming, and he could use a little extra space in the store as well.

In June 1843, Gordon thanked his friend John O'Brien for his hospitality and moved into his own house above his new store. There was another reason to celebrate. That same month, Gordon's application to the town council for freeman status was granted, meaning that, on top of all his other good fortune, he now had the right to vote.

Unlike Amasa Sprague, who was born into privilege, Nicholas Gordon had established himself as a self-made man. He had been determined to rise above the mass of poor Irish immigrants, and he had done so. He wanted the same opportunity for his family. He decided to build an addition on his store and add some rooms to his house to meet the demand for the shelter of his family. Construction started in May and was just about complete when he began to notice that several patrons were now coming to his store a tad intoxicated. An Irishman can hold his liquor, Gordon thought, "but these lads are not buying their alcohol from me." He looked into it and found that Job Wilbur was selling alcohol in his store without a license. Gordon complained, causing a great deal of consternation on the part of Wilbur, who decided to confront his old acquaintance. In June, Wilbur traveled to Gordon's house to express his displeasure, calling Gordon's action "a cheap trick." Nicholas admitted that it was but said that he was tired of being blamed for people showing up for work drunk or leaving work early to get a drink. Despite the implications, the discussion was a rather civil one with "no particular bad words between them."

But while Wilbur and Gordon were refraining from the display of any hostilities toward each other, Amasa Sprague was not feeling so generous of spirit. By June, he had had just about enough of his employees' shenanigans and decided it was time to act. He blamed the problems on Gordon and organized an effort to defeat Gordon's liquor license renewal, asking one of his trusted employees, Charles P. Searle, to appear before the Cranston town council to formally oppose the application. At their June 1843 meeting, Searle stood at the appointed time and notified the council that he "was there at the request of Mr. Sprague because the licensed establishment was having a bad effect upon the workmen who were running there all times of the day and night, neglecting their duties and getting drunk during working hours." Nicholas Gordon was furious and objected loudly. He may have thought he was able to convince some members when the council voted to postpone action on the remonstrance rather than reject it outright. Perhaps, Gordon thought, he would be able to demonstrate to the council members that it was another establishment and not his at which Sprague's employees were buying their drinks. In reality, and totally unbeknownst to Gordon, the action to postpone the vote was taken in response to an administrative error caused because the petition had been written in pencil rather than pen.

Gordon's mind was quickly occupied with more pressing matters, however, when on June 20, 1843, he met his entire family on their arrival from Ireland to the shores of New York Harbor. According to manifests, they had arrived on the *Hottinger* a day earlier. One can only imagine the pride that burst within the heart of Gordon knowing that he had experienced his American dream and was now able to share it with his family; or that of his mother in seeing her son make it in a new land and become so successful that he was able to provide that same opportunity for his entire family. What a wonderfully joyful celebration it was for an entire family, who just a few years before thought they had said their final goodbyes, to be reunited as one in America, with a world full of opportunity and promise before them. The entire family would now have the chance to lift themselves from the poverty and peasantry of their homeland and find jobs, integrate with society and become a valued part of the American culture—they would become American citizens.

Within a few days, the travelers, though exhausted from their trip, were back in Providence and enjoying a most pleasant reunion. Happiness abounded as all the Gordons knew that they would be "able to seek, in this more favored land, employment, which is denied in [their] own country." They literally had nothing but the clothes on their backs, and the clothes of John and William were quite shabby. Nicholas was all too happy to loan them some of his clothes. With the exception of William, who was a tailor by trade, none of the Gordons had a skill. But in America, that mattered little. Opportunity was everywhere, and they knew they could find employment with little trouble so long as they were willing to work hard. In fact, they did find work rather quickly, John in the dye shop of the Day Brook Mill in Johnston, Robert as a casual laborer and William as an unskilled worker in a Providence tailor shop. Though capable of more, William didn't mind starting at the bottom and proving his worth. Margaret would soon labor as a domestic servant in Providence. Initially the entire family lived with Nicholas, and all were grateful to do so until they were able to support themselves.

The exuberance of reunion, however, would soon be shattered by the life-altering political realities that were about to send all of their lives into a tailspin. In July, the Cranston town council was once again entertaining the renewal of Gordon's alehouse liquor license. This time Amasa Sprague, who had served as the town clerk from 1839 until his election to the general assembly, was leaving nothing to chance as he intended to lead the opposition himself. Charles Searle was standing at his side when Sprague leveled the accusations against Gordon, blaming him for all the drunkenness he had seen in his mill. Searle supported Sprague's allegations and presented a remonstrance signed by many villagers. One such villager who signed the petition was local boardinghouse owner Richard Knight. The Knight boardinghouse was located near Sprague's mansion and took in millworkers. He claimed to have inside knowledge of where his boarders were acquiring the drink. After hearing from the complainants, the council immediately voted, in unanimous fashion, to deny the renewal of Gordon's license. In an instant, Nicholas Gordon's generous flow of income was radically altered and many believed that he blamed Amasa Sprague.

Nicholas Gordon may have not been afforded the last word at his hearing, but he wouldn't be denied the same for the night. He turned to Sprague and, pointing a finger at him, said that he would have his revenge. Knight thought that the Irishman was worrisome and warned Sprague that he should be careful. But in his jovial way, Sprague just laughed it off, as if to dismiss the warning out of hand.

The entire family felt for Nicholas, and each tried to do what he could to help out. John Gordon was the first to take a job. Day Brook was located just across the Pocasset River that separated Johnston from Cranston and was only a short twenty-minute walk if you cut through the Sprague farm. He worked with Patrick Hawkins, who on occasion boarded with Benoni Waterman. Though unskilled, John quickly learned the ropes of the dye shop and helped the madder dyer about his works. Madder is a red substance that has a dried blood–like appearance when it stains the clothing. A man working in the dye shop could not help staining his clothes, so John frequently wore his buff vest on the job. To avoid stains he sometimes worked in his shirtsleeves. Despite the preventative measures, however, all his shirts were stained.

Sometime between August and October, William moved out of Nicholas's house and took an apartment in Providence. Having accepted a job in Dennis O'Brien's tailor shop on Back Street, he decided it would be easier to board with O'Brien at his house. At the same time, he could help ease the overcrowding burden the family had placed on his brother. Margaret also wanted to ease Nicholas's burden and announced the day after William moved out that she too would be leaving. She had taken a job as a domestic servant with John J. Stimpson of Providence and would be moving there. Nicholas felt a need to protect Margaret and strongly objected to her leaving home, but she would hear none of it. While Nicholas knew that the family would not live together forever, he was no less upset at the cause of their division.

Though no longer living under the same roof, the Christmas holiday would see everyone together at the same table once again. It was a time for merriment and celebration, and no one knew how to make merriment better than the Gordon brothers. By late morning John was already full swing into the celebration when he was spotted in the middle of the Cranston Road, some three miles away from his house, lying flat on his back and feeling the effects of several shots of whiskey. His feet were in the air, and he struggled to stand, at each attempt identifying a new way of falling back down and pretending to be much more inebriated than he actually was. John's brother William was not too far ahead. Joseph W. King, one of the village residents, had a good laugh as he rode toward the two of them on his way into Spraguesville. He loaded both of them onto his team and drove them to Nicholas's house. The pair were nearly incoherent but did manage to tell King that "they had been having a social cut," news that did not come as a surprise to him.

Margaret Gordon passed by her brothers on her way from Christmas service. It was about two o'clock in the afternoon, and the boys were heading into town. By the time they arrived home, Patrick Morrison and Michael O'Brien, two of the Gordons' friends, were already at the house, having been invited for Christmas dinner. The two were engaged in a lively conversation with Ellen Gordon, who had returned from Christmas Mass only a short time earlier at about half past two. John walked in dressed in his dark blue-black pantaloons and wearing a dark blue coat with gilt buttons. After a few words of greeting, he announced that he was going to go fetch a turkey. He grabbed a gun and headed out the door in the general direction of the Fenner place in Johnston. A couple hours later, he returned clutching a turkey. His clothes were dripping wet and his face bruised as if the turkey had been winning a fierce battle before Gordon was able to kill it. Only after he took an ax to the turkey's head, splattering blood over his already soaked pantaloons, did he agree to change his clothes. Ellen and Margaret certainly took notice that John was beaten, wet and bloodied. "What in the world happened to ya," Margaret asked in her Irish brogue. John explained that he had fallen by the side of the bridge in the swamp while chasing after the turkey adding, "I'd liked to have killed myself" as he turned to go upstairs to change and hang his wet grey pants to dry. A few more shots of whiskey were all that was needed to numb the pain, and the feast left no doubts that it was well worth his efforts.

Over the course of the next week, life went on as usual with each of the Gordons tending to their individual lives and chores. Nicholas returned to the home of Abby King and retrieved a trunk of his old clothes that he'd been meaning to take back to his house. John, still smarting from the bruise above his eye, returned to the Fenner place with his gun as if looking for the turkey's relatives to extract his revenge. Abner Sprague Jr. watched as he approached. "You're going after them, hey?" he yelled as Gordon walked closer. "Yes," he answered, pointing toward Amasa Sprague's crib a little more than quarter mile up the path. "I saw about a dozen partridges there the other day." Abner thought that strange. He'd lived there for a long time and hadn't ever remembered seeing a partridge in the area before. Perhaps the stupid Irishman was just confusing partridges with quails.

Abner was still out working his land at about half past three or four o'clock when he noticed Gordon returning from the hunt. "Did you see those partridges out there?" he asked tongue in cheek. "No," Gordon replied leaning on his rifle, "but I saw some rabbits over there."

"It's dangerous leaning on your gun like that," Abner advised. John took the gun up and opened it slightly. "It won't go off," he said, showing Abner that it wasn't loaded. The two laughed, and John headed off for home.

Neither John nor Abner could have known, but the Gordon and Sprague families were on a collision course with destiny, a course created by the confluence of four totally unrelated events that created the perfect storm of circumstance for what was about to take place.

SECTION II

DECEMBER 31, 1843:
THE DAWN OF A GLORIOUS DAY

Chapter 5

BETWEEN EIGHT O'CLOCK IN THE MORNING AND NOON

The sun shone brightly through his windows as John Gordon peered outside. Although it was only eight o'clock in the morning, John could tell by the deep-blue sky that this would be a beautiful day. Michael O'Brien stopped by to see if Nicholas wanted a ride into the city for Sunday Mass, but John told him that Nicholas was already gone.

"What happened to your cheek," O'Brien asked, "it's all swollen."

"Had a fall," is all he said. "But, hey, I'm going to Mass. I'll ride with you into the city and tell you all about it."

Before even reaching the Providence line, the two met an acquaintance, Martin Norton. It was about that time that Gordon noticed that he'd split his pants. "Mike, see how my pantaloons are busted," he quipped. O'Brien looked and laughed, noting that the split was pretty bad. "Here, take my coat," he said. John slipped it on. It was a darkish color coat and pretty long, especially on the much shorter frame of John, so it hid the tear nicely. John slipped the coat on and was still fixing the turned-in collar as he and Michael rode past another villager, James Sheridan.

For his part, William Gordon was hanging around Dennis O'Brien's house where William was still boarding. He dressed in his blue frock coat, silk velvet vest, blue pants and his hat, the same outfit he had worn every day since he had first taken residence with O'Brien. Peasants didn't have the luxury of an extensive wardrobe, so it wasn't at all unusual for immigrants to wear the same outer clothes every day. Like his brother and friend, William walked

The first Saints Peter and Paul Church was located in the Hoyle Square section of Providence. It was the church attended by the Gordon family and many other Irish Catholic immigrants in 1843. It later became the cathedral of the newly formed diocese in 1844, and a much larger building was erected on Fenner Street in Providence. *Reprinted from* Catholicism in Rhode Island: The Formative Era *by Dr. Patrick Conley and Matthew J. Smith.*

out into the bright sunshine and headed to church.

When the first Mass was celebrated at the Church of Saints Peter and Paul on November 4, 1838, the small wooden structure located on Christian Hill in Hoyle Square just outside of Olneyville was able to provide for the spiritual needs of all the Catholics living in the area. Their numbers had not yet warranted a separate diocese for the Providence area. In fact, it wasn't until 1844 that the number of Catholics flourished and a new diocese was formed with its See at Hartford, Connecticut, under the direction of Bishop William Tyler. Bishop Tyler elected to reside in Providence as the majority of Catholics from his diocese lived there. The growing Irish Catholic immigrant population, however, soon rendered the original Church of Saints Peter and Paul too small. By 1872, the Catholic population in the diocese had grown to two hundred thousand, justifying then Bishop McFarland's call for the creation of a new diocese in Providence. Pope Pius IX answered that prayer in 1871 by creating the Diocese of Providence, which encompassed Rhode Island, southeastern Massachusetts and Martha's Vineyard. He named Irish-born Father Thomas F. Hendricken its first bishop. In 1878,

Bishop Hendricken presided over the laying of the cornerstone at the new cathedral of Saints Peter and Paul, built in its present location at 30 Fenner Street in the Cathedral Square.

On the day in 1843, however, the small church in Hoyle Square was one of only a few Catholic churches in the state, and its varying Mass schedule, depending on the time of year, was certainly adequate for the Catholic population, which stood at about 2,500. In the winter months Mass began at noon and lasted anywhere from an hour to an hour and a half depending on the length of the priest's sermon.

Most of the Gordon family, and many of their friends, prayed together at the noon Mass on this beautiful Sunday afternoon, completely unaware that the events that were to follow the service would be, for the Gordon family and many others, unimaginable in every way possible.

Chapter 6

Between Noon and Half Past One
in the Afternoon

William Barker and Bowen Spencer were friends. They had been for some time. It wasn't unusual for Spencer to visit his father on Sunday afternoons, and on this beautiful Sunday, the last day of 1843, Barker left his home in Providence to join Spencer on the walk. He arrived shortly after noon, and the two talked for a while before heading out under the deep blue skies that blanketed Cranston. Spencer lived a fair distance from his father, and the walk generally took him along the same path each week, beginning from the back of John Barion's place on Christian Hill and continuing through Olneyville along the Johnston Road, past the Carpenter house and on to the senior Spencer's home.

There was nothing particularly unusual about this day. The sunshine warmed their path through the several inches of snow that covered the ground and felt soothing as it eased across their faces. Their talk and laughter made the trip seem relatively short as they occupied themselves with reminisces and funny stories. A little before two o'clock, as they passed Dr. Bowen's house, they noticed two men, one of whom was at John O'Brien's house. As they continued on just past these houses, they encountered two more men walking toward Providence. One was much taller than the other and wore dark clothes and a short coat. The shorter man carried a gun and wore a light-colored, long frock coat that went all the way to his knees. He also wore a hat and held his head high. A third man followed not far behind the first two, but Barker couldn't be sure if the three were together. The strangers were walking across the field toward the barway and passed through it and onto the road just as Barker and Spencer reached the Carpenter place. The short man came face-to-face with Spencer as he stepped out from the field and onto the track where the snow was packed hard from the foot traffic. In an unspoken game of chicken, neither man wanted to step off the path and into the higher snow on either side to allow the other passage. Each man held his ground, causing one to brush by the other as they passed. Barker and Spencer finally reached their destination and shared a cup of tea with Spencer's father.

Jeremiah Bagot lived in a house next to the Catholic church on Broadway in Providence. Although he had occupied the property as a tenant since 1839, it wasn't until a couple years before that he had been able to purchase the house, realizing his own American dream. As he did on most Sundays, Bagot rose early, dressed and tidied the house in anticipation of the Gordons weekly visit. He had known John for only a short time but had been friends with Nicholas for about seven years, and over that time the two had gotten rather close. Both Nicholas and John usually stopped by before or after Sunday Mass and shared a drink or just talked about the week's events. This day was no different, and as if on cue, John appeared at the door. He seemed a little more hurried than usual, perhaps running late for Mass, and after an exchange of pleasantries, he asked for a copy of the *Boston Pilot* for his brother. Bagot generally purchased his own copy of the Irish newspaper in the city, and because it wasn't widely available in Cranston, Bagot would generally grab an extra copy for Nicholas. John thanked him with a playful nudge, folded the paper, tucked it into the pocket of his overcoat and left for church.

Just a few moments later, Bagot also walked out, closing the door behind him. He walked briskly the few hundred yards to the church, taking in all the warmth the sunshine had to offer and, arriving at his destination, stepped inside the archway surrounding the large wooden door. Dipping the tip of his fingers into the Holy Water font, he gave himself the Catholic blessing and took his usual seat in pew eleven. As he peered across the center aisle, he noticed his friend John Gordon, who sat just ahead of him in pew ten, and acknowledged him with a polite smile.

Mass let out a little earlier than expected, and Bagot wondered if he still had time to get to the post office before it closed. On Sundays, the post office didn't close until one o'clock, and he knew it had to be close to that now. He hurried out the door but made it only as far as the corner before meeting Nicholas Gordon. The two chatted briefly, and Bagot, figuring that he could go to the post office another day, invited his friend to join him and Michael O'Brien at his home for dinner, an invitation that Nicholas eagerly accepted. The two turned and walked back to Bagot's house. As they reached Richmond Street, the church bells began to chime, letting everyone know that the one o'clock hour had arrived.

Bagot, Nicholas and Michael O'Brien, the brother of the tailor in the city for whom William Gordon worked, were just about finished with dinner when there was a knock on the door. It was William Gordon, who had stopped by to say hello. It was about half past one when a still-seated Bagot waved him in. William remained only about five minutes before the three men walked out together. Work hours were long during the week, so the Irish friends typically "made the rounds" on Sundays, visiting, however briefly, with those they didn't get to see that much on weekdays. This New Year's Eve day provided even more reason to do so.

Chapter 7

BETWEEN HALF PAST ONE AND HALF PAST TWO IN THE AFTERNOON

Michael Halohan also attended the noon Mass on New Year's Eve 1843 and took note of William Gordon sitting in church during the service, but he didn't have a chance to speak with Gordon because he had to hurry home right after Mass to prepare dinner. Gordon would be joining him for the meal, and their friend Michael O'Brien had promised to stop by for a drink as well. Halohan lived on Pond Street, not too long a walk from the church. By the time O'Brien walked up the path to the Halohans' door, William Gordon was already standing there. "Going in?" O'Brien asked with a smile. "I don't care if I do," Gordon laughed, and the two went inside. Halohan was much friendlier with John Gordon, but he knew William well and considered both to be very honest and peaceable men.

When dinner was prepared, Gordon sat by the stove, and O'Brien, Halohan and his boarder, Jeremiah Ryan, also took their seats around the table. The four laughed and told stories throughout dinner, and though Halohan had no pocket watch or clock in his house, he recalled the Sunday school chimes ringing, announcing that two o'clock had come and gone. He stood and declared that he had to attend a funeral and needed to take his leave lest he be late. Gordon stood as well and said that he would also be on his way. It was Sunday, the day that he generally visited his mother, and on this particular day, she was feeling under the weather. William didn't want to miss the visit. As William left for the walk home that would take him through Hoyle Square, and Halohan made his way to the funeral, Ryan and O'Brien continued their chatter at the dining room table.

Nehemiah White was well acquainted with John Gordon certainly enough to recognize him by sight. As he was walking alone along the Cranston Road he saw Gordon riding home, presumably coming from church.

Ellen Gordon was not feeling well but did not have the luxury of resting. She needed to prepare dinner for her family. On this day, the fare would include salt beef, turnips and potatoes—her son's favorite. John Gordon returned home from church at about two o'clock. When he entered the house, his mother immediately noticed that he was wearing another man's coat.

"What's that?" she inquired.

"I shifted my coat on account of my pantaloons being torn," he answered. "O'Brien thought the split looked bad and offered his coat for church." John took the coat off, threw it over a chair and disappeared upstairs to change into his gray pants. Once changed, John returned to the kitchen and sat, talking with his mother as she finished preparing dinner. The two ate and talked for a while longer. Ellen was enjoying the time with her son, for although they lived in the same house, his workday was such that he seldom had time to talk at any length. The sun was pretty low in the sky when John left the house. He walked out, carrying nothing in his hands and wearing the same clothes he had been wearing when he had gotten dressed in the morning, with the exception of the torn pants that he had changed. Ellen would not see him again until about seven o'clock that night.

Just down the road from the Gordons' home, at the Sprague mansion on Cranston Road, dinner was served. Amasa Sprague sat with his wife, Fanny, who was celebrating her forty-fifth birthday, and their four children—Mary Anna, Almira, Amasa and William. The children teased their mother about her age, and everyone enjoyed the merriment. Yet Amasa was preoccupied with thoughts of business. The weather was cold, and he was certain that the wind was blowing across his farm. Sunset would see a significant drop in temperature, and the damage the cold might cause certainly strained his mind. He needed to check the mill to ensure that the fires in the boilers would provide the necessary heat to keep the equipment safe. Likewise, his livestock were free grazing on the farm about a mile away, near the Johnston line, and had no barn in which to take shelter from the cold. They needed to be checked, and he wasn't comfortable entrusting the job to his tenant farmer. He had always been the type of hands-on man who preferred to tend to these details himself.

Fanny knew of his concerns and also knew that he frequently would walk to his farm on Sunday afternoons, but she had hoped that this one Sunday would be different. In addition to its being her birthday, it was New Year's Eve day, and their guests would be arriving in just a few hours.

Chapter 8

BETWEEN HALF PAST TWO AND HALF PAST THREE IN THE AFTERNOON

By half past two, Amasa Sprague was getting fidgety. He walked outside and went around to the back of the mansion toward the boardinghouse only to return a very short while later and enter through the back door. He fumbled around the house for a while, but the anxiety wouldn't leave him. At about three o'clock, he could no longer sit still. He rose from his chair, walked across the living room and stepped out into the cold, windy late afternoon air. He passed by the door of John Heap's house on the lane, or the driftway, as it is called. He reached his mill a block or two away and looked around, eventually making his way to the furnace room, which was located opposite the mill store. He arrived at about 3:20 and, once there, spoke to Edward Coil, the Cranston resident who was in charge of the fires. Sprague conveyed his fear that there might not be enough heat maintained by the boilers to operate the steam engine on Monday morning after sitting idle all day on Sunday. Coil assured him that all would be fine. The two spoke for a while longer, and at about 3:25, Sprague left the mill and walked along the private path just west of the print works, toward Carpenter's place, to check his cattle. It was a more direct route, albeit less traveled, and he took it often. As he walked the path between Hawkin's Hole and his cousin Abner Sprague's farm, his eye caught sight of Abner feeding his pigs. Because the two were so far apart, no words were spoken, and Amasa continued on his way. He was about one hundred yards north of the swamp at that point. The time was about half past three.

Above: The Sprague Mill complex consists of several buildings. This is a 2012 view of the original mill building showing the top portion of the bell tower that was added years after the mill was built. *Photo by the author, 2012.*

Left: This is the path leading to the footbridge that may have been taken by Amasa Sprague as he walked to his farm on the day of his murder. *Photo by the author, 2012.*

John O'Brien lived in a small house on the Johnston side of the footbridge that crossed the Pocasset River, which established the border between Johnston and Cranston. It was such a beautiful afternoon that he decided to go out gunning and left his house. He headed straight into the field where, at about the place of the haystacks, he overtook a man standing by a large oak tree under the bushes by Dyer's Bridge. He strained to see if he recognized him. He didn't, but he must have made the fellow feel uncomfortable because the stranger recoiled when he saw O'Brien looking his way.

Others noticed the man too. James Stratton also lived in Johnston just over the Cranston line. From the vantage point of his window, he could see part of the way over Dyer's Bridge. Earlier when he was standing by the window admiring the way the sun glistened off the snow covered field, he had noticed a man coming around the brow of the hill by Rodney Dyer's house, maybe an eighth of a mile away. The man was fairly short—at least shorter than Stratton was—and pretty stout. He wore a black hat of common size and carried a gun. The man put his shoulder against a tree and remained there for some ten or fifteen minutes, causing Stratton to think his behavior odd. The man then continued on toward the bridge at the brow of the hill until he found another tree to lean on. All told, the man hung around for about an hour and remained in plain sight the entire time. Stratton also watched as John O'Brien, whom he recognized, walked by the strange man, who never even bothered to move as O'Brien passed. "What a lazy gunner," Stratton thought to himself, "He'll be hard pressed to shoot anything today!"

Francis McClochlin lived next door to Stratton, and he, too, saw a stout and taller man leisurely walking in the potato field along the stone fence going toward the ledge of rocks. There was a tree obstructing McClochlin's line of vision, so he didn't bother to watch for a very long time and, instead, returned to his work, not thinking anything unusual about it. About fifteen minutes later, he was startled by the distinct sound of very loud gunfire.

Chapter 9

BETWEEN HALF PAST THREE AND
HALF PAST FOUR:
MURDER IN THE AFTERNOON

Ann Gleason peered out the window of her home in Hoyle Square, taking note of the sun sinking lower in the western sky and with it the unforgiving cold taking hold. From the warmth of her living room she could see Nicholas Gordon near Saints Peter and Paul Church.

Preacher Soloman E. Riley had just concluded his sermon at Rodney Dyer's Schoolhouse where he held his weekly service. Today's rousing sermon began at two o'clock and lasted well over an hour, closer to an hour and a half. As Elsie Baxter exited the front door of the schoolhouse, she saw a man walking on the footpath. Catherine Cameron also caught a glimpse of him despite the great distance between the schoolhouse and the path on which he walked.

Amasa Sprague, meanwhile, continued on his journey. He could feel every gust of the icy wind snap against the flesh of his cheeks. Adjusting his collar upward, he quickened his pace, hoping to hasten his journey so that he could check his stock before the sun had completely disappeared from the deep blue afternoon sky.

It was about four o'clock when Sprague reached the String Bridge, the footpath that crossed the Pocasset River. As he crossed into Johnston, Sprague saw from the corner of his eye a man approaching him from his left side. As the he came closer, Sprague saw the man pull a gun from his coat and point it at his head. Raising his arm in a defensive posture, he felt

Early photo of the Dyer homestead. At the time of Amasa's murder, the building was also used as a church and school house. The structure dates to around 1736. *Photo from* Cranston *by Lydia L. Rapoza and Bette Miller.*

Stone stanchions of the footbridge where Amasa Sprague was brutally attacked and murdered on December 31, 1843. This photo was taken from the Cranston side of the bridge. *Photo by the author, 2012.*

the sting of a lead ball pierce his right forearm at about the knuckle of his wrist almost at the same time that he heard the sound of the gun blast. The bullet drilled a four-inch-long path through Sprague's forearm, coming to rest just prior to exiting at the wrist. Reacting to the severe rush of pain, he instinctively reached for his right arm with his left hand, turning as he did to head back toward the Cranston side of the bridge. He staggered toward the bridge in an effort to escape his assailant, but as he did, Sprague felt a crushing blow on the back of his head and then another. The first strike knocked the hat off his head and opened two nearly parallel gashes on the upper back of his head, each measuring about an inch in length. The second hit opened a three-inch wound that started at the point of the first gash and extended backward to one inch above the ear. Almost as if forgetting the pain of his bloodied forearm, Sprague turned and tried to grab the man with his still useful left hand. Sprague was uncommonly stout, measuring just under six feet and weighing almost two hundred pounds. He was a very athletic man of determined courage. Yet the assailant made the skirmish seem insignificant. The assassin reached out with his left hand, grabbing Sprague by the chin. As he did, he lifted his right arm and, with the gun firmly in hand, brought it down hard on Sprague's upper forehead, splitting the left side wide open with an inch-and-a-half gash, cracking the skull and lacerating the membrane, causing brain matter to spill out while spraying blood in all directions. Dazed and losing consciousness, Sprague continued his struggled to get away, staggering toward the edge of the bridge but collapsing to his knees about fifteen feet short of reaching it. Sprague could feel the warmth of his own blood streaming across his icy face. Sensing that there was still life in his victim, the attacker raised his arm once again and, using all his strength, slammed the gun down against the front of Sprague's face. There was an audible sound of crushing bones, and the force of the blow broke the gun into several pieces, shattered Sprague's nose and caused a contusion that extended from the cheekbone to the temple. The temple bone now depressed the cheekbone together with a large portion of bone that had once formed the right side of Sprague's forehead. Sprague collapsed into the snow. He could no longer feel the pain of his wounds but could detect the life ooze from his body as he took his last breath, his shattered nose partially buried in the snow, his hands pinned under his massive frame.

By about four o'clock, Michael Costello had completed his shift at the Sprague mansion where he was employed as a servant. He walked out the front door and was immediately stung by the cold wind that greeted him. He had about a one-mile walk to his home, which was in Johnston on the old Plainfield Turnpike. Closing the front yard gate behind him, he turned right on Cranston Road and headed toward the mill. However, with the sun setting, he decided to take the shortcut. He turned right before reaching Nicholas Gordon's house and then walked north on the road to the schoolhouse, where he turned left. He followed the cartway, or driftway, across the swampy area called Hawkin's Hole and up the hill to the footbridge over the Pocasset Brook on the Cranston/Johnston town line. The packed snow made the bridge slippery, and he held the rail tightly with his right hand as he crossed, clutching his dinner pale with his left. He was looking down at his footing when he noticed blood splattered in the snow from the middle of the bridge to its end. It was about a quarter past four.

Joseph Cole had been visiting with his brother John who lived on Atwells Avenue in Providence and decided that he should be getting home. It was about a quarter to four, and the walk to Knight's boardinghouse on the Cranston Road where he lived would take about a half hour. John agreed to walk part of the way with him, and Joseph told him again how Amasa Sprague had promised him work at the mill and how much he looked forward to it.

Walking alone now, Joseph passed by the house across the street from the arsenal. He thought that he recognized the man walking toward him as Nicholas Gordon. Joseph slowed his pace and thought about turning around before Gordon recognized him because he owed him some money for things he had purchased in the store. Having been out of work for a while, he didn't have the money and was embarrassed to confront Gordon. He thought better of it, however, and eventually mustered up the courage to approach the man, who turned out to be Nicholas's brother, William. William laughed and identified himself, telling Cole that he was a tailor who worked for Dennis O'Brien. The two had a conversation about wages as each man proceeded on toward Knight's. The two arrived at Knight's boardinghouse at about half past four, but William was enjoying Cole's company and invited him to his house. Cole was grateful but noted that "it was against the law," and he didn't want to do anything to jeopardize his anticipated job at the mill. William looked confused, and Cole explained that Amasa Sprague had issued a directive that none of his workmen were allowed in Nicholas Gordon's store. William laughed, and the two parted company, Cole going into Knight's boardinghouse and Gordon continuing on to Nicholas's house.

John Kingston had been entertaining guests on Sunday afternoon at his home just about three quarters of a mile from the Sprague mansion, but at about four o'clock, those friends, Benjamin Earle and others, left. Not more than five minutes later, John Gordon stopped by to visit his friend John and John's brother William, who both worked at the Sprague Mill. Gordon was going to attend a christening in Olneyville later that evening and was dressed in a grayish topcoat that went to his knees, grayish trousers and boots. John Kingston had never seen Gordon's coat before and asked if he had recently acquired it. The three friends talked for a time and after a short while, left for Monkeytown to get a start on their New Year's Eve celebration. It was a beautifully clear night as they made their way over the snow-covered ground, which now crunched under the weight of their boots. The three men went into King's Tavern, where, over the course of the next hour, they had a couple drinks and made several toasts. The three then left for the return trip to the Kingston house where they would spend the next couple of hours.

Chapter 10

BETWEEN HALF PAST FOUR AND SIX O'CLOCK IN THE EVENING

It was about sundown when Nicholas Gordon and John O'Brien arrived at the christening. William H. Greene, the clerk at Tillinghast Almy's store, saw them pass by on their way. William Gordon was also expected at the christening but had yet to reach his mother's house for their visit. He had been trying to get there since Mass let out about three hours earlier, but each effort was thwarted by the chance meeting of a different friend with whom he stopped to have a drink. Now, just a few hundred yards from his destination, he bumped into yet another friend, Thompson Kingston. Kingston had left Peter Carrington's house at the end of Providence, opposite Cranston Street, in enough time to get back to the Sprague mansion before dark. It was along Cranston Street that he came on William Gordon. Kingston and Gordon chatted for five to eight minutes before Gordon told Kingston that he had come out to see his mother, who would be upset if he didn't do so. After the visit, he said, he intended to head directly to the christening for which he would surely be late.

It was very close to sundown when Joseph Cole finished his supper. He then walked onto the front porch, where he lit his pipe and sat down to smoke it. He was looking up at the starlit early evening sky when, at about half past five, not more than an hour after arriving home, Richard Knight came home with news of Amasa Sprague's murder. Cole was astounded at the news and naturally felt for Sprague and the family he left behind. But he also selfishly wondered if the demise of Sprague would also mean the end of his hopes of beginning work at the mill.

Michael Costello made his way to the end of the bridge following the path of blood to a body lying face down in the snow about fifteen to eighteen feet beyond the bridge. The large pool of blood around the man's head was a good indication to Costello that the man was already dead. Costello stared at the body for several seconds but did not recognize the battered man whose face lay buried in the snow. Rather than disturb what he suspected was a crime scene, he continued on straight to the Carpenter house where Dr. Bowen lived. He saw a man drawing water and informed him of the discovery. The man told him that Dr. Bowen would be back soon and would go check it out. Costello then continued on, first to Mr. Thornton's house and then to his own house before deciding to go back to the crime scene.

Dr. Israel M. Bowen, having been informed of the location of the body by his employee, arrived at the scene with another group of neighbors. A large crowd had already assembled and begun a search of the area for evidence. By the time Bowen arrived, the entire crime scene, with the possible exception of the body, had been substantially altered. He noted the body was lying face down, resting on the hands, the head pointing west. He gently turned the body over and, to his horror, discovered it to be that of Amasa Sprague. He immediately sent word for Robert Watson, the coroner, to officiate the dead body. The thirty-four-year-old coroner for the town of Johnston was attending a half past five meeting in Olneyville about two miles away. The meeting was just about to begin when word reached him that Sprague's bludgeoned body had been found. He hurried out of the meeting room in a rather excited state without explanation.

Watson arrived at his home to gather the supplies he would need for his work at the bridge. Realizing the significance of what he was about to do, he contacted the town sergeant, who immediately began to round up a jury, the group of witnesses who would attend as the cause of death was determined and pronounced.

Walter Beattie was one of the neighbors who walked to the footbridge to see the body. He took note of the blood scattered in drops some sixty to eighty feet up the hill on the footpath. He also noticed that none of the water, neither below the bridge nor in the river, was frozen. There seemed to be too many people walking around the area searching for clues as to what happened for him to be of any help. He left the scene.

This footbridge stanchion taken from the Johnston side of the bridge clearly shows the area where evidence of the murder of Amasa Sprague was found in the days following the murder. *Photo courtesy of Michael DiLauro, 2011.*

With the search for evidence about to be called off because of darkness, Stephen Mathewson found a pistol on the Johnston side of the bridge lying partly under it at the right side, very near the piece that sticks in the ground to hold the bridge up. The gun was full of snow and just a few yards from the body. He turned the weapon over to look at it but did not pick it up. He surmised that it might have been dropped or had fallen in the same way. He yelled to the others. Albert Waterman took charge of the gun at the scene, lifting it out of the snow. He discovered that the pistol was loaded but had been jammed with a wad of what appeared to be a piece of a Boston newspaper. He carefully unloaded the gun and put it in his pocket.

Chapter 11

BETWEEN SIX O'CLOCK AND
EIGHT O'CLOCK IN THE EVENING

John Gleason and other guests at the christening were just about to begin eating when William Gordon arrived. It was about a quarter past six, and William had finally made the intended visit with his mother. Wearing the same clothes that he wore to Mass earlier that day, William took his seat next to his brother Nicholas and began to eat his meal. William was very much the sociable type and knew how to be the life of the party. Not disappointing anyone on this night, he sang two very pretty songs as the others listened at first and then joined it.

Coroner Watson arrived at the String Bridge at about the same time as the town sergeant and the members of the jury he had empaneled. Watson examined the body and determined the cause of death. By this time, darkness had set in, and a small lantern provided the only light. So, rather than explore the entire body, Watson examined only those wounds described by Dr. Bowen.

It was now well after six o'clock, and John Gordon was just finishing up the last of his drinks with the Kingston brothers. They placed their empty glasses on the bar and departed King's Tavern. Shortly after the men arrived back at the Kingston house, the Kingston sisters ran into the house. "Did you hear about the murder?" one asked. "Amasa Sprague was beaten to death in Johnston," the other quickly added before waiting for an answer. One of the sisters and their brother Thompson worked as servants and lived at the Sprague mansion. Thompson had been in Providence all day and had not heard of the murder until told by his sisters. Immediately, Thompson, his two sisters and their mother left for the mansion to pay their respects. John Gordon walked with them to the gate but did not enter, instead continuing on to his own house just up the road.

Amos D. Smith, one of the jury members assembled at the crime scene, took note of the clothing on the body of Amasa Sprague. He and another jury member, Mr. Harris, examined the pockets of his pants and overcoat and noted the contents: a silk handkerchief, an apple, an envelope and some loose change. The envelope was clearly marked $100, but inside, only $60 was found. The two inferred that Sprague must have used the other $40 prior to his murder, leaving only what remained in the envelope. Also in his pocket was a rather expensive gold watch. The information was shared with the other jurors, and the consensus was that the murderer had taken nothing. With the coroner's examination complete, the body was released to friends and neighbors. It took several men to carefully lift the lifeless corpse and place it on a wagon before the driver then made his way back to the mansion where Fanny Sprague, her children and several well wishers waited.

Robert Watson and the jury members still had much work to do. They retreated to the home of Dr. Bowen just a short distance away. There, one of the jurors, Able Waterman, examined the pistol. He used his penknife to carefully remove the wad of paper that had jammed it. It was a piece of the *Boston Pilot*, an Irish Catholic newspaper that could readily be found in Providence. The gunpowder and ball were placed into a phial to be handed to the examining officer at the state prison at a later time. The jury then began to address the motive that could lead one to commit such a dreadful act. Because the murderer stole neither the watch nor the cash, robbery was instantly ruled out. Based on the position of the wounds, the coroner determined that some unknown person had come up from behind Sprague and knocked him off the bridge with a heavy blow to the head. Further, he concluded that the pistol and the struggle in the snow suggested that the person had an accomplice.

The team pulled up to the Sprague mansion at about a quarter to eight o'clock. Several people milled around outside. Some of them began to cry as they watched the body being taken off the wagon. Others were there more for the spectacle than because of any relationship with the family. Several men carried Sprague's body into the house through the front door and carefully laid it on the floor of one of the front parlors. One of the neighbors grabbed a pillow and gingerly placed it under Sprague's still bloody head and shoulders, propping them up slightly. Fanny cried despairingly at the sight of her husband covered in blood and barely recognizable. The children were accompanied from the room.

Chapter 12

BETWEEN EIGHT O'CLOCK AND
TEN O'CLOCK IN THE EVENING

Michael O'Brien gave William and Nicholas Gordon a ride from the christening to his brother Dennis's house, arriving at about half past eight, but after a short while, wishing to extend the evening, William decided to walk to his mother's house from there. "Don't be out too late," Dennis yelled to him as he walked out the door, warning that tomorrow promised to be a very busy day at the tailor shop for both men.

At nine o'clock, Fanny Sprague decided that she wanted Amasa to be examined by her own doctor and sent for Dr. Lewis L. Miller. She was angry and confused with many unspoken questions filling her head. Why did Amasa have to leave the house at all that day? Was it so important to check his cattle on her birthday despite the fact that several guests were coming to dinner?

Dr. Miller arrived at the mansion about a half hour later to examine the body but couldn't reach any specific conclusions about the time of death. The manner of death he concluded to be a blow to the head with a blunt instrument, probably the edge of a musket guard. The breech of the gun could have caused the fatal blows to the skull on the left temple.

William Gordon arrived back home at half past nine, having decided in retrospect that it was too cold to make that long walk to his mother's house. About twenty minutes later, Michael O'Brien offered Nicholas Gordon a ride back to his house. Gordon gladly accepted, also preferring not to walk on such a cold night. As they passed by the Sprague mansion, they commented about the large crowd still gathered outside. O'Brien had first heard of the murder while drinking at Hoyle Tavern. There were a great many people at the tavern, but none spoke openly of the murder. Although Sprague had employed Michael O'Brien for some four to five years, he didn't really care for the man and was not about to shed a tear over his demise.

It was about ten o'clock when the two men approached their destination. Gordon asked if O'Brien wanted to stop in for a bite to eat. O'Brien declined, noting that it was far too late. As he directed the team's horse to move along he waved to John and Ellen Gordon and William's little girl who had come to the window when they heard the noise from the cart.

Section III

A STUNNED COMMUNITY REACTS

Chapter 13

MONDAY, JANUARY 1

A "Most Atrocious Murder"

The ringing in of the New Year also carried with it the news of the murder, which belied the warmth of the beautiful sunshine that adorned that morning. The *Providence Journal*, the local daily newspaper, printed a prominent story under the headline, "MOST ATROCIOUS MURDER." In addition to telling the events of the murder, the story also speculated that William Sprague, Amasa's brother, would "immediately resign his seat in the United States Senate."

That is how details of the deed first reached William and Dennis O'Brien. "Mr. Sprague!" William said from behind the open newspaper, "I can hardly believe that Mr. Sprague is killed!" Many customers and friends who stopped by O'Brien's tailor shop that morning had pretty much the same reaction, and it was the topic that dominated the day's discussion just about everywhere. As much as possible, Gordon tried to avoid the excited discourse, choosing instead to focus on his work because he wanted to leave a little early in order to meet his mother to see if she wanted to go to the church on High Street for the Holy Day of Obligation. (The Catholic Church celebrates six Holy Days of Obligation each year. New Year's Day, the eighth day of Christmas, is dedicated to the commemoration of Mary, Mother of God, and Catholics are required to attend Mass. The Holy Day of Obligation originated in the seventh century. It was known as the "Anniversary of St. Mary" and called "the first Marian feast of the Roman liturgy.")

The bright sun was beginning to melt the snow that covered the crime scene by the time Walter Beattie returned to it. Nonetheless, he was able to discern

Henry Bowen Anthony was the editor of the *Providence Journal* at the time of Amasa Sprague's murder. An ardent anti-Dorrite, Anthony served as governor of Rhode Island (1849–1851) and United States Senator (1858–1884). *From the author's collection.*

two distinct sets of footprints leading in different directions. One led directly to the swamp while the second was across the meadow and led to Dyer's Pond and beyond toward Rodney Dyer's house. Beattie abandoned that trail and decided to follow the other. These tracks looked to be those of a man who took longer steps than a normal stride, perhaps indicating a running step. He remembered seeing the same tracks yesterday going from the fence near the bridge to the swamp. Each footprint was about three feet from the last, and Beattie thought to himself how unusually long a step that would be for a short man. After a couple of hours, the search was abandoned again but resumed shortly thereafter at which time Beattie followed another set of tracks to Hawkin's Hole where he now noticed even a fourth set. Another townsman, Alfred Wright, who had joined Beattie in the search for clues, noticed that the river was frozen over about fifty yards below the bridge though he wasn't sure how hard the ice was. Perhaps it only froze overnight. If so, the morning sunshine would melt it completely or, at the very least, render it unsafe.

Later in the afternoon, the Cranston Town Council met in a special emergency session to discuss the political and social implications of Amasa Sprague's death. Councilman Sheldon Knight chaired the meeting at which the council authorized the establishment of a $1,000 reward for information leading to the arrest and conviction of the murderer(s). It further resolved that the entire community had a duty to "ferret out the perpetrators of this atrocious murder that he or they may be brought to justice." In response, vigilance committees were established in several school districts. A central committee to receive and correlate all the information received by the vigilance committees was also established. Before the meeting adjourned, the council learned that the Sprague family was also offering a $1,000 reward for the conviction of the perpetrator(s).

William Gordon arrived at his mother's house to see if she wanted to go to church. However, her cold had gotten much worse than it was at Christmas, and she decided to stay in for the day. Both John and Nicholas had left a while earlier to pay their respects to the Sprague family down the street. As they returned to the store, the Gordons were completely unaware of the legal events taking place on that day.

By six o'clock in the evening, the vigilance committees were hard at work, and rumors of Nicholas Gordon's threat against Amasa Sprague several months earlier were being widely circulated. As Nicholas and John tended the store,

High Sheriff Jabez J. Potter, and a group of his men, paid the Gordons a visit. Nicholas was outside as the entourage approached, and Potter informed him that he was being arrested for suspicion of the murder of Amasa Sprague even though not one shred of evidence had been found linking Nicholas to the crime. Apparently Potter believed that an allegation of a threat alone was justification enough to make the arrest. Potter quietly walked Nicholas back into the store and tightened a pair of handcuffs around his wrists. John had been sitting by the door near the stove all this time and didn't noticed the men until Mr. Chaffee, one of the sheriff's men, put a hand on his shoulder and told John that he was there to arrest him. Potter then informed John that he, too, was his prisoner. At that point, a third member of the squad, Augustin Ellis, heard Potter instruct his men to search the store. Ellis latched the back door, preventing anyone from entering or leaving from that entrance, then walked around to the front of the store and stood by that door until the search was completed. It was no secret that Nicholas owned guns, and finding them should have been one of the primary objects of the search. But despite the fact that a pistol was on the shelf behind the counter in relatively plain view, no gun was found. Neither was anything else of any substance.

As the search of the store was still underway, James Sheldon, yet another of Potter's men, went upstairs to search the house. He found some dirty clothes in the chamber. Under the bed, he found a pair of very wet, light-colored calfskin boots that were starting to dry. John Gordon acknowledged that they belonged to him. In addition, the men found a bayonet and sword in the garret. Although the search team took note of these items, nothing was confiscated.

On leaving the store, Nicholas shut the door leading to the house and bolted it on the shop side, saying he didn't want anybody to go in. The window shutters were all fastened on the inside. Locking the door, he put the key in his pocket. As if he had not been told of the charges leading to his being led away in handcuffs, Nicholas asked why he was being arrested. For the second time, Potter told him that the arrest was for suspicion of the murder of Amasa Sprague. Chaffee noticed the large bruise on John Gordon's face and inquired about how it came to be. John hesitated momentarily and then said that he came into town on Christmas day and fell down going home. John told the men that he lived with his brother Nicholas and tended his store when Nicholas was away. John was hesitant to talk, not sure what, if any, information he should volunteer. But when he heard Nicholas tell Potter

The January 2, 1844 arrest commitment of Nicholas S. Gordon signed by Sheriff Potter. The entire Gordon family, including the family dog, was arrested before even one piece of evidence linking any one of them to the murder was found. *Courtesy of the Rhode Island State Archives.*

that he had been somewhere else on the day of the murder, John chimed in, "Yea, I can prove I was somewhere else. I went into town for a meeting and after that I returned home." Without an acknowledgement from Potter or his men, the brothers were taken to the jail.

After hearing of his brothers' arrest, William Gordon sat with his daughter and his mother. Panic filled their eyes as William tried to console his little girl. William's mind raced. He knew that because his brothers were suspects in the murder, the house would be more thoroughly searched to find weapons. He was all too aware that in his own country, where few people in the poorer classes possess arms, finding weapons in the house of a suspect is almost enough to ensure a conviction. He believed his brothers to be innocent of the crime and thought that it would be greatly to his brothers' advantage to conceal the gun. He rose from his chair, putting his daughter into his mother's arms, and entered the store, where he caught sight of the rifle that Nicholas had bought from Tillinghast Almy. He instantly returned to the kitchen door, which he had left partly open, and closed it; and then taking the gun, he carried it upstairs into the garret. To his left he noticed that there was carpet covering the floor. He tore up the cloth carpeting between the two beds that stood there and tried to loosen one of the floorboards with his fingers. He couldn't budge it. Looking around, he discovered a crooked piece of iron that looked suitable for the job. Jamming the iron between the cracks of the floorboards he forced up the end of one of the boards and thrust the gun in as far as it would go. The gun was not yet wholly out of sight, however, so he began to raise the next board. In doing this, the board split, but he was nevertheless able to accomplish his purpose. Afterward, he returned to his mother and daughter, never speaking a word of what he had done.

William had no way of knowing that he had just hidden the one piece of evidence that might have proved his brothers' innocence. In his desire to ensure that the mere act of gun ownership would not lead authorities to a wrong conclusion, he may have done his brothers as big a disservice as the *Providence Journal* was about to do them.

Chapter 14

TUESDAY, JANUARY 2

Suspects Are Rounded Up Even as Evidence Is Being Gathered

Most everyone in Spraguesville was reading the morning paper at first light. The lead story contained the gory details of the coroner's inquest, noting at the beginning that the coroner's report "failed to elicit evidence to fasten the suspicion of [the Sprague] murder upon any individual." Yet by the article's end, reasons were provided for why the Gordons, who had been arrested on suspicion of murder, were most likely the culprits. The article also falsely reported that Nicholas Gordon "ha[d] been seen repeatedly, within the last week, with a gun in his hand, near where Mr. S. [Sprague] was found."

William Gordon had not gotten much sleep. He awoke restless and concerned about a pistol that he had seen Nicholas carry on many occasions. He quickly dressed and by eight o'clock in the morning had returned to the store. There he found lying on the upper shelf a small pocket pistol. He recognized it as the one that he had often seen in Nicholas's possession. This he immediately took up and, for the same reason that had actuated him to conceal the rifle, proceeded to secret it away also. He carried the pistol upstairs in hopes of finding a suitable hiding place. It was then that he noticed the hole in the floor through which the stovepipe from the shop passed. Finding a cavity between the joists under the garret floor, he inserted the pistol. He used a yardstick to push it in as far as he could.

About this same time, Walter Beattie, a villager by the name of Dave Lawton and other volunteers were back at the swamp scouring its east side where they had previously lost the tracks. One of the men, Luther Mason, was able to pick up the tracks again, and they all followed them. Lawton was walking a little behind the others when something in the swamp caught his eye. He walked into the water and recognized it to be a coat. It was bottle blue in color and was lying in the thicket. He yelled to the others as he lifted the coat from the ground and exited the swamp. As he came out on the upland, he handed the coat to fellow searcher Theodore Quinn and quickly returned to the swamp in search of additional evidence as the others examined the coat. It was a short frock that was well worn and had a good deal of what appeared to be blood on the breast and right elbow. There was a hole on the elbow and the blood-like substance on the lining around it. As the group began to gather around, one noted the presence of wax and black hair sticking to the dried "blood." He excitedly pointed out his discovery to the others. Quinn grabbed the coat for a closer look then handed it off to another member of the search party, Alexander Boyd, who examined it and reached into the coat pockets, pulling from the right one a box containing powder. Realizing the magnitude of their discovery, Boyd replaced the items in the coat pocket and carried the coat, not to the sheriff's office, but to the Sprague mansion where they described the details of its discovery, pointing out the evidence as they did so. Lawton, meanwhile, remained in the swamp.

At the mansion, Boyd handed the coat to Rollin Mathewson in the presence of Charles Searle and many others who gathered at the house. Mathewson initially put the coat under the sofa but shortly thereafter picked it up and carried it upstairs.

On one's suggestion, the men quickly returned to the scene to resume their search, this time focusing on the left path leading to Hawkin's Hole. While some walked along the path, they heard the excited shout of another. "The gun, the gun," the man yelled over and over, "I found the gun."

Nathan Pratt had arrived at the swamp between nine and ten o'clock, entering a few rods east of Harkin's Hole, and joined some other men. They had walked through the swamp to the point of the murder, giving a good search of the river up and down each side of the stream. The group of searchers then had gone to the pond not far from the tracks. They had examined the bushes on the west side of the pond and then crossed over to the east side. They were continuing to look in the bushes when, at about one hundred yards in, Pratt had come to a tree with a hollow spot at the bottom.

He had bent down and seen the piece of a gunstock. As he bent to pick it up, his eye had caught sight of the gun barrel standing up on one end and leaning partly against the tree as if it had been tossed into the bushes and had not had a chance to fall down. It was then he gave his excited shout.

The underbrush was very thick in that spot, and he carefully reached into it to lift the barrel out. He looked around the spot a bit more before hurrying back to his house, with the gun parts in hand, where he could perform a thorough examination of it. Beattie and the others followed him there and all took a close look at what they believed to be the murder weapon. There was clear evidence of blood on the gun, but unlike the coat, no hair was discovered. Pratt turned the gun parts over to High Sheriff Potter.

As the search was taking place, Sheriff Potter had ordered the arrest of William and Robert Gordon and their mother, Ellen, on suspicion of murder. William was not aware of this order when he went to the prison at Providence Cove to try to visit his brothers in the hopes of telling them that he had hidden the guns. He was worn, tired and unshaven, but the prison guards had no intention of letting him see John or Nicholas. Once they refused him access, Gordon began to walk home. He didn't get too far before Potter caught up with him and placed him under arrest. Like his brothers, he would be committed to the prison for later examination, but first, Potter planned on bringing him by carriage to Dr. Bowen's office. Gordon complied with Sheriff Potter's order without objection. He walked to the carriage and got in. He said that he could prove that he had been, not in Cranston, but in Providence all day Sunday. Potter reminded him of his constitutional right to remain silent, but Gordon spoke freely as if he had nothing to hide.

Alfred Wright and John Shaw of Potter's staff were already in Dr. Bowen's office when Potter led Gordon inside. Gordon immediately approached Wright, mistaking him for a magistrate, and confided that he wanted to be committed. He more than likely figured that was the only way he might be allowed to see his brothers. When questioned by Wright as to the reason for such an odd request, Gordon refused to answer. His state was by now rather excited, causing others to think that he might have had something to drink although he did not in any way appear intoxicated. Gordon told Wright that he was not there on Sunday. Wright took the word "there" to mean the place of the murder. Probing for more answers, Wright told Gordon not to worry about witnesses. "Your brother [Robert] has been discharged on his own statement." "By God," Gordon responded, "that was a question of my own asking." Gordon continued to explain that he had been by St. John's Church at ten o'clock on Sunday morning and had attended a christening at about six o'clock in the evening. He gave no accounting for the time in between but insisted that he had not been in Cranston.

With William in custody, an entourage of men, including Shaw, Charles Searle, Richard Knight and others, drove a team to Nicholas Gordon's house. Their presence startled Ellen Gordon, and they told her that they needed to search the house. At first, she didn't want to let them in but then thought better of it. Ellen was confused and still feeling rather sick. She had no knowledge of William's arrest. Shaw spoke to her for a bit, and then she left the men alone in the room to conduct their search. She noticed that Shaw was trying to gain entry to the store and told him that he ought not go in there because Nicholas had locked it and had the key in his possession. Shaw immediately grew suspicious and would not be deterred. He broke the door down. A very upset Ellen accused him of wanting to steal something as if not realizing the significance of what was happening.

As Shaw and some other men searched the store, Knight, Searle and another man named Sheldon continued to rifle through the rooms upstairs. Entering what was termed "the man's room," they found the bed tumbled as if it had been slept in. The two noticed a few drops of blood on the under sheet near the head. They also found and examined various articles of clothing under the bed. Unlike the "woman's room," where there was a basket of clothes, the man's room had no such basket. Shaw reached down and picked up a shirt with a stain on the elbow that appeared to be blood and water. In the pocket, he found a grocery bill from Tillinghast Almy's store. He also grabbed a couple of vests, a dark one with spots on it containing some caps and flint and the other a box of percussion caps, six pistol balls and some powder wrapped in a brown paper. There was a blue coat with metal buttons that was, or had been, wet; two pairs of pants—one was wet to the knees and the other dry—and a pair of common sale boots that were wet and pulled from under the bed by Sheldon. He took the boots and ran downstairs and out the door.

About the time that the men were completing their search upstairs, the group dispatched to the store was beginning to wrap up its work as well. They had found a tin box and a canister, each containing powder. The powder in the vest, the canister and the tin box were similar with no appreciable difference between them. Sheldon meanwhile returned from outside the house and informed the others that he compared the measurement of the boot against some tracks in the snow that had been traced from the swamp near the crime scene to the house. He determined that it was the same boot that made the track. Searle confiscated all the clothes as evidence, and Shaw arrested Ellen Gordon. By the time she reached the prison, Ellen was very confused, troubled and ill. She rambled on but really had no idea what she was saying.

In addition to almost all the members of the Gordon family, Michael O'Brien was also arrested because he had been seen with Nicholas on the day of the murder and was known to have his own difficulties with the Spragues. All this was done despite the fact that there still was not any hard evidence linking any of them to the crime. And, in perhaps the most bizarre twist to the entire story, the Gordons' dog was arrested on the grounds that a set of paw prints were alongside some of the boot tracks that led to the swamp. The family pet was a good old dog, as feeble and harmless a mutt that there could be. The Gordons had not known him to ever hurt any living thing. He could barely walk and didn't have a tooth left in his head. Regardless, the sheriff picked up the dog for examination. Ellen, Robert and the dog were all released later in the day.

Meanwhile, evidence-gathering volunteer Horatio Waterman was with fellow searchers John DeMerritt and George Wellman at the crime scene. They decided that with all the evidence that had already been retrieved, it would be beneficial to follow the tracks to see where they led. The task was difficult, as dozens of men had been scouring the site for the past two days, packing down snow and making thousands of new tracks. They were able to follow a set a tracks from the bridge across the bog meadow to Dyer's Pond, across the pond to the place where the gun was found, from there to the place where the coat was found, and finally from that location to Hawkin's Hole where the track was lost. At this point, the men decided to split up. DeMerritt and Wellman went over the crossing into the swamp while Waterman took a left at the fence. There he noticed tracks of a rather crooked boot, about size eight or nine, that went along the north side of the fence. He had no formal measuring device with him but instead placed a stick along the track in various places to note if it was the same track all along. The tracks were of sufficient distance apart to indicate a man running. These tracks led Waterman right to the spot where the coat was found. He continued to follow them to Hawkin's Hole where the ground was soft. It appeared to him that, at that point, the man had jumped from branch to branch. In some places the tracks had been saturated with water and frozen, making those tracks distinct.

Waterman rejoined DeMerritt and Wellman, and the three went to the orchard at the top of the hill overlooking the valley. From that vantage point, it appeared to them that the tracks went to within five or six feet of Nicholas Gordon's house. DeMerritt disagreed, saying that the track looked more to be about fifteen to eighteen inches from the Gordons' door. Because of the depth of the track, they deduced that it was made from a running step, except between the spots where the gun and coat were found, where the tracks appeared to be made by a shorter step. Although there were tracks on both the north and south side of the causeway, only one track led from Hawkin's Hole to the Gordon door.

Richard Knight had had a long day and looked forward to having his dinner with his friend Joseph Cole. The wariness from his day shone on Knight's face, prompting Cole to ask if something was wrong. Knight launched into a recounting of the day's events, telling him of the various arrests, the questioning of suspects, the searching of the crime scene and the Gordon house and store and the variety of evidence found. Of the plethora of information, Cole was particularly struck by the list of people arrested. In fact, one name in particular gnawed at him. "William Gordon?" Cole asked incredulously, "He couldn't possibly have been involved in the murder? He was with me!" Cole then recounted his chance meeting with William on the Cranston Road at the exact time that the murder was supposed to have taken place. Knight seemed distant, and his thoughts were clearly elsewhere. Cole picked up the vibe and decided not to pursue the matter, but before Cole could change the subject, Knight added in a very calm voice: "There's nothing against William." Cole took that to mean that William had been released and moved on.

Chapter 15

WEDNESDAY, JANUARY 3

Providence Journal *Shows Evidence of Bias*

The men and women of Spraguesville were immersed in the facts of the murder case at this point, and the sale of newspapers was soaring. It was pretty much all that was talked about at work, at home, in the stores and on the streets. However, the only information that the general public was privy to was what was printed by the *Providence Journal*, whose stories were becoming more biased by the day. The January 3 newspaper led with the arrests of the Gordon family and their friend Michael O'Brien. It addressed the evidence that had been found, including the gun, which the *Journal* falsely reported as having belonged to Nicholas Gordon, and the bloodstained coat with the hole in the elbow that perfectly matched the bloodstain on the elbow of the shirt found in Gordon's home. Regarding the arrest of the Gordons' family dog, a *Journal* reporter wrote: "Close to the tracks of a man found leading to the swamp, were tracks of a dog. Nicholas Gordon owns a ferocious dog, which was found in his shop by Officer Shaw, who forced the door. This dog wears a collar of jagged metal, and some of the wounds upon Mr. Sprague are such as would be made by such a collar on a dog springing at his throat. The dog is in the possession of the officers." The reporter clearly does not seem to be describing the same dog as the one owned by the Gordons.

While the *Journal* was doing its best to convict the Gordon family before a trial could be held, Dr. Thomas Cleaveland, the keeper of the jail, entered William Gordon's cell to speak with him. Under intense questioning, Gordon proclaimed his innocence and pointed to the evidence of it. Cleaveland dutifully took notes in his memorandum book but didn't really appear to be paying close attention. Gordon meticulously recounted the events of his Sunday, noting that he visited his mother at about two o'clock and stopped at the halfway house to get cider between four and five o'clock. He returned to his mother's house and had dinner before going out with some friends.

Dr. Cleaveland then went to the cell of John Gordon. He again kept notes as Gordon explained how he was at church in the forenoon and then returned home, arriving sometime between two and three o'clock. Dinner not being ready yet, Gordon went to the Kingstons' house. From there he and two of the Kingston boys went to King's Tavern for something to drink. They left the tavern around sundown and went back to the Kingstons' where they remained until they were told of the murder.

Dr. Cleaveland completed his notes, closed his notebook and left the cell.

The murder scene was still a hotbed of activity. Walter Beattie noticed that neither the water in the river nor under the bridge was frozen. Gardner Luther, another of the volunteers who stepped forward to assist with the search, used a stake to pick the snow where Sprague's head had lain and said he found several more pieces of the gunlock. Another man produced the gun tube. All this evidence was returned to the sheriff.

Chapter 16

FRIDAY, JANUARY 5

The Funeral of Amasa Sprague

Despite the disruption caused by the large crowds that had taken charge of the Sprague mansion for the past week, Fanny wanted Amasa's funeral at the house. Servants cleaned every square inch of the mansion as a large concourse of people, neighbors, friends, millworkers and citizens from other towns attended. The *Providence Journal* noted that no member of the Gordon family attended the service, something they ascribed to that family's guilt. The *Journal* continued its assault of falsehoods against the presumed guilty. It cited incriminating testimony from a ten-year-old girl who allegedly lived with the Gordons despite the fact that the only young girl who actually lived with them was the seven-year-old daughter of William, and she would certainly not have been someone to rely on for testimony. The *Journal* also wrongly identified Michael O'Brien as a child rapist who received only a small sentence for his conviction. In fact, they were describing a different Michael O'Brien, who was convicted of assault with intent to commit rape and received a sentence of four years, which he was still serving at the time that the story appeared. Journalistic integrity was clearly something the *Providence Journal* was willing to sacrifice in an effort to ascribe guilt to the Gordons.

While most of the town was preoccupied with the funeral, the Gordons were in serious trouble and needed to select their defense team. Those selected composed a "dream team" of the day. It included Thomas F. Carpenter, Samuel Y. Atwell, Samuel Currey and John P. Knowles. Carpenter, who

Above: A 2012 photo of the Sprague Mansion showing the original home on the left and the later addition to the right. *Photo by the author, 2012.*

Left: Portrait of Thomas F. Carpenter, who served as lead defense counsel for John and William Gordon during their 1844 murder trial. *Rhode Island Bar Association photo.*

would serve as lead attorney, was the Dorrite who ran unsuccessfully for governor as a Democrat in 1840 and again in 1842, as an Equal Rights Democrat. Word quickly spread through the community that such a high profile defense attorney must have been paid for through the generosity of a supportive Irish Catholic community in Providence. In actuality, Carpenter was paid nothing for his commitment but rather was taking on the task to make certain that "no man charged with a crime of murder that is on trial for his life, was convicted because there was no member of the bar willing to volunteer his services in defense of the prisoner."

Atwell, Carpenter's associate, had run for attorney general as a Democrat in 1843. Like Carpenter, he lost. He was also a former member of the legislature who supported suffrage and the abolition of capital punishment. Knowles worked in the same law office as Carpenter and, like him, was a Dorrite. Curry, a conservative, was an ardent anti-Dorrite who provided political balance to the defense team.

For its part, the state selected former attorney general W.H. Potter to assist Attorney General Joseph M. Blake with the prosecution. Like Amasa Sprague, Blake was a conservative. The thirty-four-year-old Democrat joined the anti-suffrage Whigs in the Law and Order Party. Potter was actually the personal choice of William Sprague. He was a junior partner in the law office of former attorney general Albert C. Greene. His father was a conservative member of the state legislature and congress. Blake and Potter were bitter rivals of Carpenter and Atwell in the elections of 1843, which, more than any other election before it, was wrought with fraud and corruption. To say that this case was personal to them would be a gross understatement.

With Supreme Court Chief Justice Job Durfee presiding, the stage was set for the trial of the century to begin.

Chapter 17

JANUARY 9–APRIL 8

The Two Sides Prepare for Trial

The state wasted no time preparing its case against the Gordons. Still without anything beyond circumstantial evidence, it hired S. B. Cushing, a surveyor, to prepare a plat map depicting the vicinity of the A&W Sprague Print Works, the Sprague mansion, the Gordon house and all the properties in which evidence found up to and beyond the point of the murder in Johnston. The order was to include on the map all the evidence against the Gordons so that a jury could understand the relationship between places and events. Cushing set out immediately to accomplish the task.

On Friday, January 12, John, William and Nicholas Gordon were bound over for grand jury investigation on murder charges. Sheriff Henry L. Bowen escorted the three men into court, marking the first time since their arrests that the brothers had been in the same room together. Their examination was held in secret with former attorney general Albert Greene representing the state and Samuel Currey and John Knowles appearing for the prisoners. Following the grand jury investigation, John and William were committed for trial. The examinations of O'Brien and Nicholas Gordon were adjourned until Monday.

Alfred Wright summoned James Francis to the jail to identify the gun that was found near the murder scene. Without hesitation, Francis identified it as the same gun that he had left with Tillinghast Almy for resale in his store, the one that Almy said was later purchased by Nicholas Gordon. His certainty, he said, stemmed from the fact that this gun—a small, rough-made

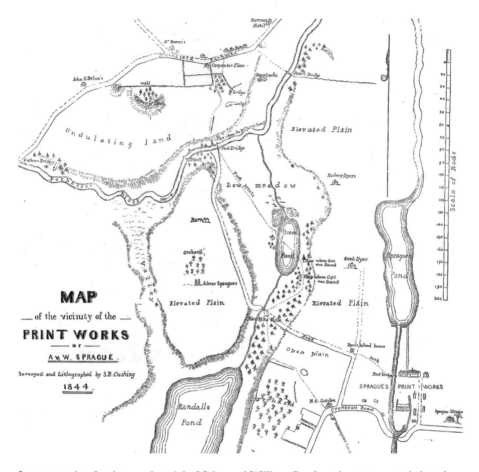

In preparation for the murder trial of John and William Gordon, the state commissioned S.B. Cushing to prepare this map of Spraguesville and the surrounding area. The map was completed by January 9, 1844, and became a crucial piece of evidence in the trial. It is a damaging visual, showing a direct path from the scene of the murder to the points where evidence was discovered and leading right to the door of Nicholas S. Gordon. *Reprinted from the 1844 trial transcript.*

fowling piece with a percussion cap lock and full stock—was unvarnished and contained brass trimmings. Furthermore, he claimed that he "would [have] know[n] [this gun] among a dozen guns by the small bore and a screw gone." Francis confirmed that he left the gun with Almy for sale in the fall of 1843 after owning it for only a short time, adding that Almy had sold it for $2.50 and paid him after the sale.

Monday, January 15, began with the examination of Nicholas Gordon and Michael O'Brien before the grand jury. As a result of the hearing, Nicholas was bound as an accessory before the fact of murder. O'Brien was discharged.

As the *Providence Journal* predicted on the day following the murder, William Sprague III resigned his seat in the United States Senate to return home and assist in the investigation of his brother's murder. He also needed to run the A&W Sprague Company that operated the print works and other family enterprises.

The trial of John and William Gordon became an urgent matter for the court. It was scheduled to start on Monday, April 8, 1844, just five weeks from then, even before that of Thomas Dorr, whose alleged crime occurred much before the Gordons'. The pressure seemed to be getting to all involved as their lives had already been irrevocably altered.

JOHN AND WILLIAM GORDON GO ON TRIAL FOR THEIR LIVES

Chapter 18

THE TRIAL, DAY ONE: MONDAY, APRIL 8

"Some Man Hath Impiously Assumed the Prerogative of His Creator"

The red brick, Georgian-style structure located at 150 Benefit Street in Providence was built in 1762 as one of five buildings to be used as a meeting place for the colonial and state legislatures. The Providence State House, as it was known, was the place where the Rhode Island General Assembly first read the Declaration of Independence. It figured prominently in some of the events of Dorr's Rebellion of 1841 and 1842, and it would be the place of his trial. This day, however, it was the site of the most notorious murder trial in Cranston's history.

Chief Justice Job Durfee entered the chamber, and everyone in the overcrowded courtroom stood on command. Durfee, an ardent anti-Dorrite, had already ruled Dorr's attempts at reform treasonous. He symbolized the social and cultural divide between Irish Catholic immigrants and the Protestant, old Rhode Island family elites. For the trial, he would theoretically sit, along with Associate Justices Staples, Hale and Brayton, as an impartial jurist in the trial that would come to symbolize that fissure.

Carpenter calmly glanced at his pocket watch, noting that it was just a minute or two after ten o'clock when Attorney General Blake moved that the prisoners be brought into court and arraigned. As if on cue, Nicholas, John and William Gordon were led into the chamber. As the prisoners entered, Carpenter moved that the three defendants be afforded separate trials allowing each to stand or fall on his own case and be unaffected and unprejudiced by the guilt or innocence of the other. Attorney General Blake immediately noted his objection saying that John and William had no right

The grandeur of the home of Samuel Y. Atwell on Putnam Pike was befitting Glocester's most prominent resident. After Atwell's untimely death in October 1844, just following the trial of John Gordon, the home became the Chepachet Inn and a setting for court trials, town meetings and other public gatherings. His law office was located just south of the inn. Both buildings were destroyed by fire in 1913. There is no known image of Samuel Atwell. *Photo from a postcard from the Providence Public Library.*

or sound reason to demand separate trials because they were each charged with the same crime. Defense attorney Atwell interrupted, "But we address ourselves solely to the discretion of the court. These men are entitled to a fair and impartial trial. It is a case of momentous importance to them. It involves their lives. The right of each prisoner to be tried by a jury of his own selection is impaired by compelling them to be tried jointly." (The defense would clearly benefit by separating the two trials for many reasons, including that there was a greater chance that perjured testimony would be more easily detectable if people not bearing truthful witness were forced to repeat their lies several times over several weeks and in different venues. However, the overriding reason was that separate trials would ensure that a jury would not be prejudiced by applying the weight of the evidence against one defendant to the other.)

Judge Durfee did not try to hide his dissent with the motion, noting that the prisoners John and William were jointly indicted for the crime, and as there was "no reason shown to the court why they should be tried separately the court thinks they must be tried jointly." The fact that the chief justice of the Rhode Island Supreme Court did not believe that the administration of justice was not in itself a valid reason to separate the trials sent a bad omen to Carpenter.

After the rendering of this decision, the three men were arraigned, and all three entered pleas of not guilty. The jury was empaneled with twenty-two jurors being peremptorily challenged by the prisoners. Six were set aside for having formed an opinion and three because of "conscientious scruples." The selected panel included no Irishmen. They were sworn in and prosecuting attorney Potter opened for the government.

Standing before the jurors, Potter began his opening statement:

> *A crime, gentlemen, of the highest magnitude, a murder most cruel and atrocious in its character, has been committed. A life most valuable has been violently and illegally taken. A citizen most worthy and respected, in the peace of God and of the State, upon his own soil and almost at his own door, the sun of whose last day had not then gone down, upon God's holy Sabbath, has been brutally murdered. Some man hath impiously assumed the prerogative of his Creator.*

The jury listened intently, and the room was still. Potter went on to describe the murder, lay out the evidence and establish that neither the state nor the Sprague family was prejudiced, noting that

> *in this prosecution the Government has no feelings of resentment, no passions to gratify…And here gentlemen, allow me to say one word in relation to the brother and relatives of the deceased, who are present attending the progress of this trial. They entertain no other feelings toward the prisoners at the bar, than such as are warranted by the proof. They desire only to ascertain the naked truth. This duty they owe to the memory of the deceased.*

Potter continued by describing the murder scene, recounting Sprague's last moments on earth and introducing a map depicting the scene of the crime and showing how the tracks and evidence trail led to the Gordons, whom he lumped together as though the entire family were accomplices. He concluded by offering his opinion of the value of circumstantial evidence:

> *Facts may be proved by circumstantial testimony in a manner as strong and conclusive to the mind as by positive testimony. Nay, gentlemen, in some*

Portrait of Governor William Sprague (1838–1839). Sprague was serving in the United States Senate when he learned of his brother's murder on December 31, 1843. *State House Portrait Collection.*

cases it may be stronger and more convincing. One, two or three witnesses swearing positively to a fact may be mistaken or deceived. They may have formed a design to deceive, they may have been bribed, or they may perjure themselves. If a fact can be proved by a number of witnesses, each one swearing to a simple disconnected fact only, the chance for combination to deceive is lessened and the means of detection are increased. When these facts, thus sworn to, all correspond, and together make up a continued chain of testimony, it is more cogent and conclusive upon the mind than any direct testimony. Its binding effect upon your consciences as jurors is by the law as great. In fact, gentlemen, nearly all the criminal cases from the very nature of the case are, and must, be decided upon circumstantial testimony. Men about to commit a crime disconnect themselves from others, and naturally seek concealment.

Immediately following his opening statement, the first prosecution witnesses were called. Dr. Israel M. Bowen led off by describing the condition of the body: "I turned the body over and recognized it as the body of Amasa Sprague…I discovered the wound on the left side of the head which had fractured the skull, ruptured the membrane of the brain, and the brain had protruded through it." The jury recoiled at his words, but he went on to discuss the other wounds he had found. His testimony was followed by that of Dr. Lewis L. Miller, the physician called by the family later on the day of the murder, for the purpose of substantiating Dr. Bowen's recounting of the description of the wounds.

Carpenter wrote furiously, noting additional points he would need to address in his own opening statement to refocus the juror's attention, conferring with Atwell as he wrote. Under cross-examination, Carpenter asked if Dr. Miller might be able to pinpoint the time of death. He could not.

Land surveyor S.B. Cushing was called to the stand and asked to describe the detail of the map that he had prepared at the request of the state. He did so in meticulous detail, noting that "the scale of distances which accompanies the plat [was] correct, and the places [were] put down in their true relative positions."

Abner Sprague, Amasa's cousin, was called to establish Amasa's Sunday travel routine. Noting that he had seen Amasa walk past his farm at about 3:30 p.m., he said that Amasa "always traveled this path when going to the Carpenter place. Amasa Sprague frequently went to the Carpenter place on Sundays; more frequently I should think than on other days."

Michael Costello was next up and explained his relationship to the Spragues as their servant at the mansion. He told how he discovered, first, some blood on the bridge and, then, a body, later identified as that of Amasa Sprague, at about sundown as he walked home from work. Day one of the trial came to an end with the cross-examination of Costello by Carpenter.

Chapter 19

THE TRIAL, DAY TWO: TUESDAY, APRIL 9

"I Might Be Mistaken about Its Being Blood"

The prosecution opened day two of the trial at nine o'clock in the morning by calling Walter Beattie to detail the pattern of the spattered blood at the crime scene. Before the second witness could be called, however, a communication was handed to the court indicating to one of the jurors that his grandson was dying. The juror's request for dismissal was granted, and a new juror, Jonah Steere, took his seat. For reasons unknown, the defense offered no objection to the unorthodox process of juror replacement. The prisoners were again arraigned and again pleaded not guilty. The attorney general briefly reviewed the evidence presented to that point in the trial, and the state called its next witness.

The Johnston coroner, Robert Watson, was asked to explain how he became involved in the case and his role in the examination of the gun: "One of the jurors [empaneled at the scene of the murder], with a pen-knife, drew the wad [of paper from the gun.] It was loaded to within an eighth or a quarter of an inch of the muzzle. I put the powder and bail in a phial, and the wad and paper by itself. I delivered the pistol, phial and wad to the examining officer at the prison. The wad appeared to be a piece of a Boston newspaper." Under cross-examination, however, Watson could not remember who first called his attention to the pistol or why. He also acknowledged that there were some fifteen or twenty men already assembled when he arrived and that the snow was "much trampled and thrown about."

Stephen Sprague lived in Cranston a mile or more from Amasa Sprague's house. He testified that he found a piece of a gun or pistol: "I found it on the Cranston side of the bridge…I picked it up and gave it I think to Daniel Dyer, I'm not positive…the blood was on the bog side of the road, and it appeared to have got over the fence into the bog…The piece [of the gun] seemed to me a sliver which had come off by the breech pin of a musket or pistol. There was blood and hair on the sliver; the hairs sticking to the sliver." Blake produced the sliver, which Sprague identified as "looking like the same that [he] had found."

Walter Beattie was re-called to describe the appearance of the ground at the place of the murder. He spoke of tracing the blood "pretty near the body and on the bridge two-thirds of the way from the end of the bridge to the water; on the path the blood went zigzag." He described, too, how the snow was trampled, suggesting a struggle had occurred, saying that "there were footprints from the place where the struggle was to the place where the body lay, and blood. Most of the blood was upon the posts which support the bridge." Blake asked Beattie to recount how it came to be that the tracks were first discovered:

> *I proposed to go home across the meadow, as it was nearer; we came a little way and found a track, a single track in the snow. I asked what it meant; it went back to the fence, and we could see it the other way as far as a track in the snow could be seen on a smooth meadow. We followed this track to the pond—Dyer's Pond. We could not see it on the ice but we saw it [the track] on the other side. We went over and found the track coming down the pond. It was larger than the other and went up the edge of the pond towards Rodney Dyer's house. We followed it a little ways and I said it was no use to follow that track, it was better to see if we could find the other track. We then went back and a little further down found a track that seemed to be the same that we had followed from the fence near the bridge. The track was of a man who took longer steps than I should do on an ordinary walk. I followed the track down into the swamp. The last I saw of it was the print of a heel on the top of a cedar bough, which was bent over. I stepped onto the same and it bore me. The next step I took I went in nearly the whole length of my leg. Here I lost sight of the track, went out upon the upland where some men were, then came back and looked again; went through the swamp and down an opening towards Hawkin's Hole. Going down through the opening I saw two tracks, but did not examine them because there were two.*

Beattie next spoke of how it came to be that the coat was found, describing in detail its appearance and the contents of the coat's pockets.

Under cross-examination, Beattie admitted that he didn't measure the tracks after he crossed the pond but rather measured the length of the steps. The defense, in an effort to show that any number of people may have made those footprints, asked Beattie to explain the habits of the five or six hundred residents of Sprague Village, to which he replied, "I don't know whether the people of this village remain at home on Sunday or not. There is not a great deal of visiting between the villages. Many of the people in Mr. Sprague's village come into town to meeting on the Sabbath; I cannot say whether there is any particular solemnity at the Catholic Church the day after Christmas or not."

The prosecution then called Walter Beattie's brother, Robert, who was also at the crime scene, for the purpose of corroborating Walter's testimony regarding the tracks. Horatio Waterman, likewise, confirmed Walter Beattie's account and added, "I went with these men [John DeMerritt and George Wellman] to the orchard on top of the hill; saw the measure laid into the track within five or six feet of Nicholas Gordon's door, and also twenty feet back. The measure was the same there as in other places. No other track would correspond to that measure except the straight one that crossed the meadow. I should think that the boot was rather a crooked one."

Carpenter rose to cross-examine this witness.

"Mr. Waterman, how can you be sure that the tracks you traced were made on the day of the murder?"

Waterman paused, then said, "I do not say that the tracks were made on Sunday."

"In fact," Carpenter continued, "can you say with any certainty that the tracks on one side of the pond were even made by the same person as those on the other side?"

"The track was perfectly distinct," Waterman answered. "There were other tracks by the side of it [the pond] but none crossing it." Not satisfied with the answer, Carpenter continued to badger the witness.

"Are you certain they were made on the same day at the same time?"

"I infer that the track was an older one, from the fact that in the wet places, it had frozen; in other places I don't know that there was any different appearance. I should think the snow would have melted a little in the open places on Monday," Waterman responded.

"And what was the distance between the place where the gun was found and the place of the coat?" Carpenter asked.

"It was seven or eight rods from the gun to the coat." Then, as if to explain why the tracks had frozen over in only certain spots, Waterman added, "The sun would shine there for an hour or two."

John DeMerritt was called to verify Waterman's testimony. He also testified that he measured the boot taken from Gordon's house against the track. "I applied the measure I had used to the boots," he explained under examination by the attorney general. When his turn came, Carpenter pounced.

"Exactly how did you measure the track against the boot?"

"I applied it to the sole of the boots," he responded. "It corresponded in length. There was about the eighth of an inch difference in the breadth. The track was about an eighth of an inch wider than the boot, ascertained by applying the measure to the sole of the boot." Then, DeMerritt made a crucial admission. Referring to S.B. Cushing's plat map, DeMerritt said, "I was with Mr. Cushing when he altered the plat, between Hawkin's Hole and the door." The alteration referred to is in a pencil mark and to the north of the darker track, going up to the door. Carpenter attacked once more.

"Why was it necessary to alter the map after it had been completed?"

"When I traced the track south to the causeway it was lost in the path made by the travelers on the driftway," DeMerritt said, "It turned out again four rods east of the place where it came on the causeway. A man other than the one whose tracks I was measuring coming along the driftway might have turned out here." Carpenter now had an acknowledgment from the prosecution's own witness that so many people had trampled the snow around the crime area prior to the measurements being taken that the tracks could have been made by any number of people. That should have equated to reasonable doubt, but Carpenter wasn't finished with this witness just yet.

"Is not the boot that was found in the Gordon home, the very one produced here that you measured against the tracks, a very common size boot?"

DeMerritt hesitated. "It is not very remarkable for men to wear boots of the same number. If the boot was the same size I do not know that I could tell whether it was worn by the man who made the track on the north side of the driftway or not. I should have supposed, if I had not seen the tracks on the other side of the driftway that the tracks on the south side were made by a man turning off from the driftway at this point."

Carpenter viewed DeMerritt's cross-examination as damaging to the state's case. Although the trial still had a long way to go, the defense had reason to be at least cautiously optimistic at this point in the proceedings.

The state called David Lawton to the stand. Lawton was the Cranston resident who had found the coat in the swamp at about eight o'clock on Tuesday morning when seven or eight men went from the store to the pond to continue the search for evidence. He said he had noticed something in the pond, retrieved it and found it to be a bloodstained coat. Carpenter began his cross-examination. "How did you come to know that the stain on the coat was blood? Did you have it tested?" Lawton recanted. "I might be mistaken about its being blood; I took it to be blood." Blake slumped in his chair and seethed.

Hoping to recoup some of its lost ground, the prosecution called Nathan B. Pratt. He stated that on Tuesday, between nine and ten o'clock, he had gone from Arnold's boardinghouse to the place where the murder was committed and searched the river. After a thorough search of both sides of the river and pond, he "found the gun to the east side about a hundred yards from the tree." The stock he found in the hollow at the base of the tree and then the barrel. "There was blood and hair on the stock," Pratt noted.

Gardner Luther was the state's next witness. He was the man who had found the gunstock, the tube and the percussion lock in the snow at the place where Sprague's body was found. He testified that he found, too, a screw head and had given everything to an officer at the Sprague house. Carpenter practically jumped to his feet. "Mr. Luther," he said as he handed the witness the gun, "is this the gun that you saw in the possession of the Gordons?"

"I do not know that Nicholas Gordon ever had this gun," Luther said slyly. "I have seen him with a gun. I think it was two weeks previous to the murder. Can't say whether the gun resembled the gun in court or not." Attorney General Blake rose to question the witness, hoping for more clarity. "Mr. Luther, did you know of Nicholas Gordon having a gun about the time of the murder?"

This was not a discussion that the defense team was about to allow to take place. Judge Durfee had already separated the case of Nicholas Gordon from that of his brothers who were now on trial. Certainly evidence against Nicholas, who had yet to be tried, could not be introduced at this trial. "I object to that question," Atwell said. "It has nothing to do with the guilt or innocence of these men whether Nicholas Gordon owned a gun or not. The Government must first prove that the gun was ever in the hands of these prisoners. Nicholas Gordon is not now on trial. The prisoners must be brought into contact with the gun."

Blake countered, "The murder was undoubtedly committed with this gun, and it is perfectly competent for us to prove the ownership of the weapon with which the death was inflicted...for the purpose of showing that the prisoners might have had access to it, for the purpose of bringing them into contact with it." Atwell would have none of it. "The Government [is] beginning at the wrong end with their proof. They ought first to bring the prisoners in contact with the gun and then they may prove whose gun it is, but they have no right to prove that this was Nicholas Gordon's gun for the purpose of inferring hence that it was used by the prisoners."

Chief Justice Durfee had heard enough. "It is competent," he said, "for the Government to prove this fact, of the ownership of the gun, in the same manner as they prove the corpus delicti. If they do not afterward connect the gun with the prisoners the evidence of course goes for nothing. The attorney may ask the question." The defense was incredulous and looked at each other as if to question whether the judge was using this trial to rewrite judicial law.

The defense team's concern was somewhat abated, however, when Luther answered, "I do not know that Nicholas Gordon had a gun, cannot say that it was this gun. I should think two weeks previous to the death of Mr. Amasa Sprague, saw him with one, can't say that it was this; it resembled this gun."

As the hour was getting late, the prosecution called Hardin Briggs as its final witness of the day. Briggs testified that he saw Nicholas Gordon with a gun last fall and described it as an old-fashioned gun altered into a percussion lock. When presented with the gun in evidence, he said, "That gun is very much like the one I saw him have, the lock of this gun has been altered from the old lock to a percussion lock."

On cross-examination, Atwell got the witness to admit that he couldn't even remember what month it was that he saw Nicholas with the gun. "Funny," Atwell noted, "that you can remember so many of the fine details about seeing Nicholas but not the time of the year that it occurred!"

As the second day of the trial came to a close, the defense team took stock of what had been proven to that point. The state had established that a prominent man in the community had been brutally beaten and murdered; that pieces of a gun were found at and near the place of the murder but that the gun could not be placed in the hands of the defendants and could not, with any degree of certainty, be placed in the hands of the defendants' brother; and that a coat was found, but it was not proven that the coat belonged to either of the defendants. The defense was even able to cast doubt that the stain on the elbow of the coat, which was assumed by the witnesses to be blood, was in fact blood. Finally, several witnesses testified that tracks had been traced from the murder scene and that some of those tracks led to the door of Nicholas Gordon. Yet, it was also established that many other tracks that led in other directions were not followed, almost as if to imply the selection of a suspect first with the subsequent gathering of the evidence needed to incriminate only the selected person. Certainly a jury would see through that, they thought. The testimony further established that tracks that led to Nicholas Gordon's door seemed to match a boot of very common size found in Gordon's house. Even if it could be proven that it was Gordon's boot that made those tracks and not one of any of a hundred other men with that same boot, such evidence would tend to incriminate Nicholas but would have done nothing to directly implicate the two defendants. Further, and most importantly, it was not even established that the tracks were made on the day of the murder. The crime scene itself had been so damaged by the significant number of men who had walked about between the day of the murder and the point at which the track evidence was gathered that there was no real proof that the tracks that were followed were even those of the murderer. At this point of the trial, they agreed, they were not faring too badly. Of course, on the downside, the jury was not to their liking, with not one Irishman being empaneled, and the judge did not seem to be presiding in a very objective manner. Still, the group was cautiously optimistic about what the next day would bring.

Chapter 20

THE TRIAL, DAY THREE:
WEDNESDAY, APRIL 10

"I Cannot Swear This Is the Same Gun"

The courtroom was already packed with onlookers when the defense team arrived a little before nine o'clock the next morning. Court began shortly thereafter with Walter Beattie being re-called to clear up some confusion about the view of the Gordon house from the Stone house. Then, James Francis, the man who had left a gun for Tillinghast Almy to sell, was sworn. He described the gun in meticulous detail and was able to positively identify the gun found at the crime scene as the exact one that he left with Almy.

James H. Sabin, the clerk from Tillinghast Almy's store, followed Francis in the witness stand and noted that on October 5, 1843, he had recorded an entry in Almy's book that read, "James Francis, one gun, settled." He noted that it was an entry for sale with Francis being the name of the person who had left the gun to be sold. Blake asked Sabin to read a second entry from the book. Sabin obliged, "(Francis, October 7, sale fowling piece), N. Gorton [*sic*]." He explained, "I recollect the gun." As it was shown to him in court he added, "I should think this was the gun, but I don't know. It compares with this. I know that the gun left by Francis is the same as that sold to Gorton, because it is so entered on the book. The name of the owner is put in the left column." Again, the defense saw an opening. "So you don't know if this is the same gun that was left at your shop for sale and which you then sold to an N. Gorton?" Atwell asked. "I cannot swear this is the same gun but have no doubt of the correctness of the entries." The defense had established reasonable doubt.

One of the state's key witnesses was next to take the stand. Sheriff Jabez J. Potter was the man who had arrested John Gordon and searched the Gordon store and house. He recalled the circumstances of the arrest and the condition of the clothes, some of which "appeared to have been quite wet but have got dry some." He spoke of the very wet boots, noting that John Gordon claimed they were his. He also discussed the bayonet and sword, which were found in the store's garret. He acknowledged not confiscating any of it at the time but noted that he did see the items at the jail at a later point. Potter added, in response to several questions, "There was a mark on John's face; did not notice it particularly; heard him say something about a fall on Christmas."

Daniel K. Chaffee, another key witness who had searched the Gordon store and residence, said that he searched the store himself and found no gun. "Looked for it particularly," Chaffee said, "as I understood a piece of a gun was found. I looked more particularly in the store than the house." He too recalled seeing the bruise on John Gordon's face. "Quite a large bruise as though he had [had] a heavy blow. I asked him how he came by that bruise. After considerable hesitation he said he came into town Christmas and fell down going home." Chaffee, like Potter, testified that there were no clothes taken that evening. During cross-examination, Chaffee said that Gordon did not ask why he was being arrested. "He seemed sullen and unwilling to converse; he was very slow and reluctant to talk."

John M. Shaw served the precept against William Gordon. He told of how he went to the Gordon house to arrest other members of the Gordon family and to search the premises again. The old woman was not cooperative and appeared very ignorant. He described the items of clothing and the powder and paper found. He particularly spoke of the wet boots and how he had measured them against the tracks outside. Atwell again rose for the purpose of cross-examination and noted that the boots were of a very common size. Shaw acknowledged that to be the case.

Tillinghast Almy, the auctioneer who sold the gun to Nicholas Gordon, was asked to testify as to the sale of the gun and explain why the "Gordon" name was spelled differently in his books. He acknowledged that he spelled Gordon's name wrong using a "t" rather than a "d."

"Both names, Gordon and Gorton, mean the same man on my books all the way through," Almy said. "There is another gun entered in June, 1842, to N. Gorton, do not know by whom left. W.H. Green, my boy, made this last entry. There is no entry by whom it was left. The other gun, the entry was to Francis, which shows that he left it there. No doubt of the correctness of the entry."

The next few state witnesses didn't seem to help the prosecution's case much. John Cassidy testified that he knew Nicholas Gordon and thought he saw a coat like that taken out of a lumber wagon at Nicholas Gordon's some six or eight months ago; however, he "never saw him wear it to [his] recollection."

John Kingston told the court that he was with John and William Gordon between four and five o'clock, before it was dark, on the day of the murder. "We went soon after to Monkeytown; got some drink at King's tavern." He recounted how they all first came to hear of Sprague's murder.

William Kingston testified that "he [John Gordon] stopped with his brother Nicholas when the murder was committed." He went on to confirm his brother's testimony adding that "there was nothing extraordinary in John's appearance, dressed in top coat down to his knees, grayish kind of trousers. Just as pleasant as ever I saw him to be. Saw no difference in him."

The final two witnesses of the day were called to show that John Gordon had access to Nicholas's guns. Abner Sprague Jr. testified that he saw John with a shotgun in his hand near the place of the murder on the Friday before. Gordon said he was going hunting for partridges over near Amasa's crib where he saw a dozen of them. Benoni Waterman said he saw John standing at the door of the store "holding something up to his cheek pointed toward the barn. I called it a pistol." He also recalled seeing John at eight o'clock on the morning of the murder and didn't recall "that he had a black or swollen cheek at that time."

Chapter 21

THE TRIAL, DAY FOUR: THURSDAY, APRIL 11

"There, You May Go Now"

A s day four of the trial commenced, several witnesses testified that they saw John Gordon on the Johnston Road in the vicinity of the murder on that fateful Sunday. The most significant of them were William Barker and Bowen Spencer. They both testified that they had gone to visit Spencer's father and were on the Johnston Road a little after noon when they observed two men, a tall one and a short one who carried a gun. When they were returning home later that day, they observed the two men once again. This time the tall man carried the gun. There was a third man behind them. One man had no jacket on and walked with his head down. Both walked very fast. They thought it odd for them to be going gunning on such a cold day and return without a coat. Barker thought he had seen the shorter man in Dr. Israel Bowen's office at the time that Michael O'Brien was being examined and noted him to be about the size of John Gordon. Spencer testified that he had seen William in jail and thought him to be the taller one. Blake felt good about this testimony, feeling that it placed John and William at the scene, but Carpenter saw the identification of the two men as the prisoners to be tentative and weak at best.

Several other witnesses testified in support of previously provided testimony, and the trial moved along uneventfully until Attorney General Blake asked Richard Knight if he was aware of any difficulty between Nicholas Gordon and Amasa Sprague. Carpenter immediately objected based on irrelevancy to the issue. "The object of introducing this testimony was to give to the prisoners a motive for the commission of this crime; but

Rhode Island Supreme Court Justice Job Durfee presided over the trials of John and William Gordon and Thomas Dorr. He will forever be known as the "Hanging Judge" because of the death sentence imposed on John Gordon. *Reprinted from* Liberty & Justice *by Dr. Patrick Conley.*

the ill-will of Nicholas cannot be presumed to have been shared by his brothers without proof of the existence of any such hostility on their part." Potter argued otherwise, saying that if the threats of Nicholas were made in the presence of the prisoners it was relevant. After a very long debate, Judge Durfee instructed the state to continue with its case and noted that he would decide the issue after the recess. Several additional witnesses were called that tried to place the coat in the possession of John Gordon.

The afternoon session began with the judge's decision on the admissibility of the evidence of threats of Nicholas Sprague made in the presence of the prisoners. To that end Durfee ruled that

> *the evidence must pass to the jury for them to judge how far such threats may have affected the minds of the prisoners so as to furnish them with a motive to commit this crime. The relevancy of it may be illustrated by supposing the prisoners should offer to prove that a most friendly and amicable relation and the kindest feelings existed between Nicholas Gordon and Amasa Sprague, the deceased, with a view of showing the absence of all motive*

on the part of the prisoners. The Court in such case would feel bound to admit the evidence.

This decision did not suit the defense at all, and Atwell noted his exceptions for the record.

In an effort to prove that Nicholas Gordon was in Providence on the day of the murder—to show that he could not have committed the crime and thereby imply that his brothers must have—Attorney General Blake called John DeFoster to the stand. Atwell immediately objected saying, "All the evidence so far goes to fix the commission of the crime upon Nicholas S. Gordon, and we say the Government has no right now to prove that Nicholas Gordon did not commit it, in order to draw an inference that these prisoners did." The reply by Justice Staples shocked the defense:

This murder was committed as the Government contends, with Nicholas Gordon's gun and Nicholas Gordon's coat. Now, if the case were to go to the jury on this evidence, would you not contend before them and with great force that Nicholas Gordon was the perpetrator of the murder? If so, is it not perfectly competent for the Government to rebut such a presumption by showing that Nicholas was in a situation where he could not have used that gun or coat, on that day, and thence we infer that the prisoners at the bar who had access to the gun were most likely to have used it?

Flabbergasted, Atwell replied, "But the Government ought first to show some connection between the prisoners and the gun and coat, before they can rightly draw any such inferences."

"I presume the Government think there has been some testimony to that point already put in," Staples replied. Justice Brayton added, "Here are three persons who have access to a certain instrument with which a murder has been committed. You wish to discover who did use it. Proof that one of these three was absent and could not have used it, is certainly proper evidence to incriminate the other two." With that, Durfee admitted the evidence.

Carpenter and Atwell were beside themselves. The three justices had essentially guided the jury in its thinking. DeFoster then testified that he saw Nicholas at 3:30 p.m. by the Catholic church in Providence. Several other witnesses supported that testimony.

The government then sought to inflict the most damaging blow to the defense by introducing witnesses that overheard Nicholas Gordon threaten Amasa Sprague in the presence of John and William. They did so first by calling Susan Field, a known prostitute who worked for Madam Susan Parr in a brothel run from 20 Benefit Street in the city. Field testified that she had known Nicholas for three years and visited his store often, as many as three times a week. She said that Nicholas owned two coats, one an old bottle blue that she had seen John wear on one rainy day. She also saw John wear Nicholas's black pants. She said he also owned two or three vests, which she never saw John or William wear. The implication was that she knew all three brothers well enough to identify their clothing and how often they wore them. She testified that she saw a pistol with a percussion lock in Nicholas's store lying on the shelf. Then she delivered the bombshell:

> *I heard Nicholas say Amasa Sprague had taken his license from him; he would be the death of him. "They took John Holloway's license from him, but Goddamn him, he shan't take mine away. I'll have my revenge. I'll be the death of him." John was present and an Irishman when this was said. The Irishman said, "No Nick, you don't mean so." Nicholas said, "Yes, by God, I do mean so. I would run him through just as quick as I can wink," and he struck his fists together. Nicholas was the head man of the family. The rest did as he said.*

John Gordon leaned over to Atwell and told him that he didn't know this woman. So on cross-examination, Atwell made sure the jurors knew of Field's profession and then reinforced her stated familiarity with the prisoners by having her describe her numerous visits to Nicholas's store. Finally, Atwell asked, "You know William and John, do you not?"

"I know them when I see them," Field's responded.

"There they both are," Atwell noted, "which is William, and which is John?"

The witness turned and pointed to William saying, "That is the one I am not so well acquainted with, that is John; that one," pointing to John, "is William." The room fell silent. All were amazed that the witness who had just testified that she visited Gordon's store as many as three times a week and knew the brothers so well that she knew when they wore each other's clothes had just misidentified the two suspects.

"There, you may go now," Atwell said with a dismissing wave of his hand. Blake swallowed hard. The witness he relied on to make the causal connection between the threat of Nicholas and the brothers had just failed to properly identify the prisoners.

William Manchester testified that he heard Nicholas make threats against Sprague but not in the presence of his brothers. Atwell objected to any testimony that pointed out Nicholas's feelings toward Sprague that were not made in the presence of John and William, and this time, not even Judge Durfee could disagree, ruling such evidence inadmissible. Hardin Hudson and John Shaw testified that they heard such threats made in the presence of John Gordon, but the vision of Susan Fields pointing to the wrong brothers during her identification is one that would have a more lasting impression on the jurors.

The attorney general then called witnesses to prove that Amasa Sprague was responsible for the council's denial of Nicholas Gordon's license renewal. With that, the government rested. Atwell half seriously teased, "We propose now, under the last ruling of the court, to summon witnesses to prove that Mr. Sprague has had difficulties with others; and, also, to show that they had an opportunity to commit the murder." Durfee was not amused when he said, "Well, sir, you can offer such evidence as you deem expedient, and if the court think it competent, they can suffer it to pass the jury." With that, prosecuting attorney Potter gave a stirring closing argument. By the end of the fourth day of the trial, the defense had reason to be sanguine.

Chapter 22

THE TRIAL, DAY FIVE: FRIDAY, APRIL 12

"Madder Makes a Stain Like Blood"

Thomas Carpenter opened for the defense knowing that he didn't need to prove anything. Rather, he needed only to dispel allegations made by the government that might tend to implicate his clients. He noted in his opening statement that his view of the case thus far was "that the only evidence which had been introduced connecting with any certainty either of the prisoners with this transaction was the testimony of Barker and Spencer implicating William Gordon," adding that the witnesses had met two men on the Johnston Road who may in fact have been the true murderers. Yet, the defense, Carpenter said, would prove that William Gordon was in Providence on the day of the murder at 3:00 p.m. To make the case, Carpenter called Jeremiah Bagot, who testified that William was at his house on that day. The testimony that William was in Providence and that John and Nicholas were also in Providence at various times of the day was supported by Michael Holohan, Jeremiah Ryan, Michael O'Brien, Martin Quick, Catherine Holohan, Dennis O'Brien, John Gleason and Thompson Kingston. All of the witnesses recounted the details of that New Year's Day and the time they spent with the Gordons during various parts of it from church in the morning to the christening at night.

In the afternoon session, the defense began to take the prosecution's case apart by presenting testimony that would dispute what had been presented by the government. First up was Tillinghast Almy, who testified that he never saw Nicholas wearing the coat that was found at the crime scene and did not recognize that coat when he was shown it in court. John Fleming,

Jeremiah Bagot, John O'Brien, William Arnold and Joseph W. King all offered similar testimony. Abby N. King testified that Nicholas boarded with her for approximately ten months and during that time naturally kept his clothes at her house. Despite her intimate familiarity with his clothing, "I never recollect seeing the coat until I saw it in the grand jury room. I have never seen it before except here."

With the issue of the coat behind him, Carpenter now focused on trying to account for the wet clothes. For that purpose, he called as a witness Margaret Gordon, Nicholas's sister, who testified that she had lived with Nicholas while she lived in Cranston and "saw part of Nicholas's clothes," also acknowledging that he might have clothes that she didn't see. However, when shown the coat found in the swamp she said emphatically, "I never saw that coat." She responded to several questions saying, "I went home the day before Christmas but saw John on Christmas day. It was two o'clock when I got home; John was there, his clothes were wet. He said he had got a fall. He went after a fowl over to Fenner's; came back in a short time [with a bird]. It was a turkey. John killed it…All John's clothes were wet; we told him to go up and change them. I suppose he went and changed them after killing the turkey. He was a little worse for the liquor." Michael and John O'Brien and Patrick Morrison all testified to the same circumstances with Morrison adding that when John cut off the turkey's head, some blood got on his pants.

Carpenter also called witnesses who cast doubt as to the cause of the red stains on John's other clothes, which the state, without ever having them tested, had tried to imply was blood. Patrick Hawkins said that he worked with John Gordon at Daybrook for more than two months and boarded with him at Benoni Waterman's until the work stopped. "He helped the madder dyer about his works," Hawkins said. "Madder makes a stain like blood; a man working there could not help staining his clothes. John seemed to be a prudent, quiet man. I recollect a vest which he had which was much stained; a buff ground. I believe a red speck in it. His shirts were stained as he used to work in shirt sleeves."

Others testified as to John's character and described him as peaceable and quiet. Another said he never heard anything against the Gordons. Carpenter glanced at Atwell, who with a nod of his head affirmed Carpenter's thoughts on the success of their first day of defense testimony. Yet there was no time to rest or celebrate. The next day, they would have to account for John Gordon's whereabouts on the day of the murder.

Chapter 23

THE TRIAL, DAY SIX: SATURDAY, APRIL 13

"Should Think a Man Might Be Seen Passing across the Field to the Back Door of the Gordons' House from the Cranston Road"

The court did not take a recess on Saturday. Instead, it commenced at nine o'clock in the morning with the defense team calling the day's first witness. Seneca Stone lived near the Gordons and was familiar with the travel customs of the villagers. He testified that people coming from Fenner's sometimes took the road that ran by his house and toward Gordon's door. "Should think a man might be seen passing across the field to the back door of the Gordons' house from the Cranston Road," he said. Furthermore, he noted that he was Nicholas Gordon's closest neighbor and had seen him as many as three times a day in all kinds of weather and "never saw him with the coat on which ha[d] been produced here." With this testimony, Carpenter gave the jury a reason to believe that the tracks going from the murder scene to Gordon's door could have been made from any villager taking that road.

John Gordon's mother, Ellen, was still feeling the effects of a protracted illness when she took the stand Saturday morning. She described John's activities on the day of the murder in great detail, accounting not only for his whereabouts at the time of the murder but also the condition of his clothing and the bruise on his face. However, under intense questioning by the attorney general, who pointed out inconsistencies with her testimony in court and her statements in prison, she appeared more of a protective mother than a credible witness. After more than an hour on the witness stand, Ellen Gordon requested leave to go out of the courtroom and into the open air. It was clear to all present that she was feeble and sickly. She was permitted to do so, which brought an abrupt end to her testimony.

Much of the balance of the day's testimony centered around prior witnesses being re-called for the purpose of clarifying their statements. One such witness was Edwin C. Larned, who took notes of the examination of Ellen Gordon at the prison. He read his jailhouse examination, which contradicted much of her courtroom testimony. Carpenter objected to the reading of the notes on the grounds that such evidence must be recalled from memory not read from notes. Gordon had previously testified that her prison statements meant nothing because she was sick and confused following her arrest and was not in control of what she was saying. The objection was to no avail as Durfee allowed Larned to read verbatim from his notes.

Day six of the trial had come to an end, and still the defense team felt positive about the way things had gone thus far.

Chapter 24

THE TRIAL, DAYS SEVEN AND EIGHT:
MONDAY, APRIL 15–TUESDAY, APRIL 16

"If You Want to Whip a Dog,
You Will Find a Stick in Every Bush"

Monday morning came quickly, and Sunday did not afford the defense team much rest. The day's initial testimony focused on casting doubt on the validity of the method used to trace the footprints. Several witnesses testified that "the snow was so beaten up we could find no tracks."

While the casting of doubt on the track evidence was an important element of the case, the critical mission of the day was to provide an account of William Gordon's whereabouts on the day of the murder to show that he could not possibly have committed the crime.

To that end, Joseph Cole was first to take the stand. Unlike Susan Field, Cole correctly identified the accused and told how he was walking with William at the exact time that the murder supposedly took place. This testimony was key not only because Cole boarded with Knight but also because he worked for Amasa Sprague and had not known William Gordon before this chance meeting. He simply had no incentive to lie. The attorney general tried to discredit the testimony during cross-examination, but the damage to his case against William was evident.

Up to this point of the trial, the defense team had debunked the theory of the blood, planted sufficient reasonable doubt on the issue of the wet and bloodstained clothes, offered reasonable alternate explanation for the tracks leading to Nicholas Gordon's house and accounted for the presence of both John and William in places other than the murder scene. The only thing left to do was to provide for someone else who could have been in position to carry out the crime. In that regard, Bowen and Spencer, the prosecution witnesses, had already established that there were two other people in the vicinity of the crime at the same time as the murder. If one of them couldn't be William, then logic dictates that the other one wasn't John.

James Stratton and Francis McClochlin were called to tell what they had witnessed on the day of the murder. Stratton began, saying that he had seen "a man coming round by the brow of the hill by Rodney Dyer's. He put his shoulder to a tree, and stayed there some time; some ten or fifteen minutes. He had a gun and was shorter than I. He wore a dark frock; looked pretty stout...I said that was rather a lazy gunner."

McCochlin's testimony was similar. He had seen "a man in the potato field walking along the stone fence, going towards the ledge of rocks. [He] heard the report of a gun afterwards...[but] could not see if he had a gun. He was a tall man, taller than either of the prisoners...He was walking leisurely from the end of the wall towards the ledge of rocks." McClochlin continued his explanation: "My testimony was taken down before by Mr. Mathewson. I did not know William, but should have known John if I had seen him in the clothes he used to wear."

Finally, John O'Brien testified that he, too, saw a man standing by the oak tree by Dyer's bridge, under the bushes. He affirmed: "I don't know who it was and he drew back when I saw him." A few other witnesses were called to reaffirm prior testimony. Satisfied with the completeness of their case, the defense was ready to rest.

In all, the trial had lasted six days, over which time 102 witnesses offered testimony. Each side provided detailed closing arguments. For his part, Carpenter pointed out the pretrial prejudice of the *Providence Journal's* accounts of events, noting that "one of their own countrymen [Mr. Cole] tells you he had little doubt of their [the Gordons] guilt from reading the statements in the newspapers." He also spoke of the fear that engulfed a community so dependent on the Spragues for their livelihood in coming forward to testify for the Gordons. "Men have been so stupid as to believe, that for them to come here and testify in behalf of the accused, would be offensive to the friends of the deceased. We have had the greatest difficulty in getting men here to testify." Finally, he implored the jury to not fall into the trap of linking the accused to the facts based on preconceptions, but rather pursue "in this case a different course. Let us trace the facts in the first place, and come to a conclusion afterwards: not seeking to confirm a previously formed impression, but seeking to find what ought to make upon the mind a correct impression." Carpenter addressed the weaknesses of circumstantial evidence, saying, "If the circumstances are such as to be consistent with only one hypothesis, they are as forcible as any evidence. The train of circumstances may be so clear and convincing that the mind has no more doubt than if a virtuous and upright man should swear that he saw the transaction with his own eyes. But there are many instances given in the books, where terrible mistakes have been made by juries relying too fully upon this kind of evidence." He then provided a few actual examples of such injustices.

He addressed the issue of motive by saying that John and William simply had no reason to take revenge on Amasa Sprague, and without positive evidence, a motive is needed. The strongest circumstantial evidence, Carpenter noted, was provided by Barker and Spencer who saw two men, a short one with a gun and a taller one, while walking to Spencer's father's house. The same two men were met on their return but this time the taller one with a gun and the shorter one not wearing a coat. Carpenter continued:

> *These men were no doubt the murderers of Amasa Sprague…and the short man, they swear, was William Gordon. This is the only link that connects either of these prisoners with any certainty with the murder of Amasa Sprague. This is the strongest circumstance in the case…But gentlemen, Barker and Spencer were mistaken. They did not see William Gordon on the Johnston road. They could not have seen him. They made that mistake which men are apt to make when suspicion is aroused against a man. Men then begin to see things which they never dreamed of seeing before. Everything is construed as guilt. As the old proverb has it, "If you want to whip a dog, you will find a stick in every bush."*

Carpenter spoke for a total of nine hours that spanned two days, finally concluding just prior to noon on Tuesday, April 16, saying, "And now gentlemen, after having thus gone into the material facts in this case, and taken more time than I had intended, I will leave the case to be closed by the able counsel who will follow me—I leave the prisoners to God, and the country, which country, gentlemen, you are."

On Tuesday afternoon, Mr. Atwell addressed the jury for the defense. He was quite ill (from an ailment that would take his life six months later) and was able to speak for only five hours, condensing his remarks accordingly. He focused his closing remarks on the role of the jury in cases based only on circumstantial evidence:

> *Now take care gentlemen, and it is this duty which I would impress upon you as men, as Christians, as citizens, as jurors, sitting there under the oath*

of God. Take care that you do not transfer your feelings of indignation against the crime, to the men who are accused of its commission. This is one of the most difficult points for jurors to overcome...Take care that you do not admit this feeling into your hearts, take care that you do not commence your consideration of the evidence with the theory, (stated by my learned brother in the opening,) that these men are guilty because they are accused, and then seek to fit your facts to that theory. It is this danger that I would warn you against. Look at these men as you would look at me or any other unsuspected individual, and then form your opinion of their guilt or innocence.

With these words, day eight of the trial of the century came to a close.

Chapter 25

THE TRIAL, DAY NINE:
WEDNESDAY, APRIL 17

"I Can Only Hope to Present the Naked Facts"

Atwell's testimony lasted until the end of court on Tuesday and continued into Wednesday morning, when he concluded with these words: "There are many things now, which I would say if my strength permitted. These men are strangers in this country; they are poor and unfriended. I have endeavored to do my duty by them—that duty which I never shrink from in a capital trial if God gives me health and strength. It is yours, gentlemen, to do the rest. In your hands are the lives of these prisoners. I commit them to your protection, and may 'God Almighty send them a safe deliverance.'"

With that final plea, the defense of John and William Gordon came to an end. Attorney General Joseph Blake, over a period of five hours, meticulously summarized the government's case, concluding, "But the prisoners have been defended by those of their counsel who have addressed you, with consummate ability, and commanding eloquence. In following such counsel, I can only hope to present the naked facts plainly before you, so that you may come to a conclusion from the impression they are calculated naturally to make, and not unwarily confound the creation of the genius of the advocate, with the testimony of the sworn witnesses on the stand."

It was now Justice Durfee's obligation to charge the jury and provide instruction on how they must conduct their deliberations. This is a routine part of judicial proceedings, and no one expected much by way of controversy. Yet Durfee used the opportunity to foster the growth of anti-Irish prejudice, the seeds of which had previously been planted and that had already taken root within the Yankee population.

Durfee began by explaining the significance of circumstantial evidence, noting that much of what is considered positive evidence turns out to be circumstantial on critical examination and that the two are equally conclusive. He then offered "some views in regard to the most essential part of the evidence in this case." Here, Durfee spoke of the importance for the jury to consider each prisoner's opportunity to commit the crime as well as the potential that he used that opportunity. Then, Durfee began to cross the line of judicial discretion. First, he implied that the testimony of John Gordon's mother was not credible:

> *If you believe the mother of the accused he clearly had not* [the opportunity to be present at the murder]. *But you will have to estimate the credit to which she is entitled, and in doing this, you will necessarily consider the relation in which she stands to the accused; her manner of testifying here; the consistency of her story with undoubted facts in the case; her declaration to Mr. Knight, made a day or two following the murder, as to the time of John's absence, what he said on his return; and her evidence given before the magistrate, and read here by the witness who took it down in writing; and if you should not consider her entitled to credit here on the stand, then the question of opportunity must be decided by other reliable testimony in the case.*

Discrediting a witness for the jury was bad enough, but Durfee apparently felt that there was too much still left to chance. He added:

> *A word as to weighing testimony and I shall have done. If witnesses be of equal credibility and have equal opportunity to know the same facts, and they contradict each other, no legitimate inference can be drawn from their testimony, and leave the mind in doubt. If witnesses be of equal credit, but one has a better opportunity to know the facts than the other, that one must be believed in preference to the other. Questions of identity are often questions of belief. I say this in reference to the testimony relating to the gun, the coat, the pistol, and some of the testimony in relation to persons of the Gordons. So questions of time are also questions of belief, where a person has no artificial means of measuring it, and in all these questions, we must be governed mainly by the belief and opinions of those who are the best able to judge, or have the best opportunity of judging, and their judgment may be rectified and reconciled by those undoubted facts in the case which make up the great body of the evidence.*

The defense team was once again incredulous. The judge, the chief justice of the supreme court of the state of Rhode Island, essentially just told the jury to put greater emphasis on the testimony of the Yankee villagers than on that of the Irish Catholic immigrants, a message that was not at all lost on the all-Yankee jury. He further insinuated that if the Irish immigrants were too poor to afford a timepiece, then greater credibility should be placed on the testimony of those who had such an instrument. Today, jury instructions such as these, wrought with judicial prejudice, would, at the very least, be grounds for a new trial if one were needed.

Chapter 26

THE VERDICT: WEDNESDAY, APRIL 17

"It Is You, William, Who Have Hung Me"

With Durfee's reverberating judicial challenge, the jury retired to an anteroom for deliberations, and the court recessed pending its verdict. The hour was six o'clock in the evening, and Carpenter spoke to his clients briefly before they were led away, reassuring them that they had a good chance of winning acquittal based on the evidence presented during the trial. Yet as he walked off, he bowed his head and must have wondered if the facts presented at trial, coupled with the judge's instructions, would be of sufficient weight to sway the jury members toward a verdict of not guilty.

He would not have to wait long for his answer. At a quarter before eight, with the jury having deliberated for only an hour and forty-five minutes, Carpenter was summoned back to the courtroom. A verdict had been reached. Carpenter knew that such a quick decision did not bode well for his clients, but as they reunited in the courtroom, they just sat stoically and looked straight ahead. No words needed to be spoken as the jury members filed into the room and took their seats. The court clerk faced the jurors and asked sternly, "Have you agreed upon a verdict?"

"We have," foreman J. C. Hidden answered.

The clerk then inquired, "Gentlemen of the jury, who shall speak for you?"

"Our foreman," was their unanimous and choreographed reply.

The clerk turned toward John and William Gordon and instructed, "Prisoners, look on the jurors." John glanced at William. His heart sank low in his chest and he trembled with anticipation as he turned to face the twelve men who held his very life in their hands. "Jurors, look on

The October 9, 1844 commitment of John Gordon to prison where he would be held until his execution on February 14, 1845. *Courtesy of the Rhode Island State Archives.*

the prisoner," the clerk continued. "What say you, Mr. Foreman, is John Gordon guilty, or not guilty?"

"Guilty," the foreman answered. John felt his knees begin to buckle. As the importance of their words began to take hold the clerk asked, "Gentlemen of the jury, as your foreman hath said, so do you all say?"

"We do," the jury answered in unison.

Before William could even digest what had just taken place, the clerk turned to him. "Prisoner, look on the jurors. Jurors, look on the prisoner. What say you Mr. Foreman, do you find William Gordon guilty?"

"Not guilty," the foreman said. There was an audible gasp from the men who had assembled to view the proceedings. The clerk recorded the verdict and finished, "Gentlemen of the jury hearken to your verdict, as the Court have recorded it. We find William Gordon not guilty. Is that your verdict, gentlemen?"

"It is," they replied.

"William Gordon, you are discharged," Judge Durfee said. As he said this, John looked at his brother, exclaiming, "It is you, William, who have hung me." Carpenter looked bewildered and wondered what he meant, but before he could ask, John was bound and led away by the sheriff.

Present in the courtroom throughout the trial were reporters from the *Providence Journal* and the *Boston Pilot*, the official newspaper of the Archdiocese of Boston. Each paper had a very different slant on the proceedings and each reporter a very different reaction to the verdicts. Over the course of the next few months, each would take advantage of the opportunity to present their individual reactions.

Chapter 27

POST TRIAL:
APRIL 18–OCTOBER 9

"I Further Declare, That I Never Knew That Gentleman"

What started out as one family's dream of a better life in America morphed into the nightmare that had just unfolded. As most Irish immigrants of the day did, the Gordons had come to this country with the goal of working hard and escaping the depressing economic and social conditions that had plagued their homeland. Nicholas found the true meaning of the American dream by developing and growing a business, owning his own home and flourishing enough to enable him to reunite his family in Rhode Island. No one had forewarned him about the anti–Irish Catholic sentiment he would find here, and no one could have anticipated the horror that such prejudice would inflict. But life for the entire Gordon family, indeed the very tight-knit Irish Catholic community itself, was now irrevocably and forever altered.

While John Gordon's hope had depleted, his attorneys and the Gordon family persisted in their efforts to bring justice to this most unwarranted course of events. The day following the verdict the defense attorneys filed a motion to defer John Gordon's sentencing until after the trial of his brother Nicholas. While Samuel Atwell's now serious illness was cited as one reason for the filing, the overriding reason for the request for a delay was that the trial of Nicholas might reveal previously unknown facts that may serve to exonerate John. William Potter opposed the motion noting that Nicholas Gordon had ample time to reveal any facts pertinent to his

THE TRIAL

OF

JOHN GORDON AND WILLIAM GORDON,

CHARGED WITH THE

MURDER OF AMASA SPRAGUE,

BEFORE THE

SUPREME COURT OF RHODE ISLAND,

MARCH TERM, 1844:

With all the Incidental Questions raised in the Trial carefully preserved—the Testimony of the Witnesses nearly verbatim—and the Arguments of Counsel and a Correct Plat of all the Localities described in the Testimony, prepared expressly for this Report.

REPORTED BY EDWARD C. LARNED AND WILLIAM KNOWLES.

PROVIDENCE:
PRINTED AT THE OFFICE OF THE DAILY TRANSCRIPT.
MARCH, 1844.

[SECOND EDITION.]

PROVIDENCE
SIDNEY S. RIDER.
1884.

There was so much interest in the trial of John and William Gordon for the murder of Amasa Sprague that the trial transcript was published in 1844. *Image from the author's collection.*

brother's innocence during John's trial but chose to remain silent. He added that a swift hanging would serve as a deterrent to other criminals and as an example to all.

To no one's surprise, Judge Durfee agreed with the prosecution, adding that he would entertain a petition for a new trial if the prisoner's counsel wished to submit one by the following morning. The next morning, John Gordon was led into court, and Attorney General Blake moved "that sentence of death…be pronounced upon him." Defense attorney Knowles countered with a petition for a new trial, moving that the hearing on the petition be postponed until the October term of the court due to absence of Attorney Atwell, John Gordon's lead counsel.

"The prosecution presented evidence of Nicholas Gordon's hostility to Amasa Sprague without first proving a conspiracy," Knowles argued and cited, furthermore, that "notes of Ellen Gordon's testimony before the examining magistrate were allowed to be read even though the witness stated that he had no recollection of the testimony itself." Durfee ruled in favor of the postponement, agreeing that there was no time to take the matter of an appeal up during this session of the court and continued the matter until the afternoon of the first day of the October. This represented only a hollow victory for Knowles as it would appear that the hearing would still take place before the trial of Nicholas Gordon in mid-October.

Tensions continued to rise in the days following John's verdict. Emotions in the Irish community also ran high as the trial of Thomas Dorr commenced just eight days after John's trial had ended. On May 1, 1844, one of Amasa Sprague's two sons was accosted and severely beaten. The *Providence Journal* immediately identified his attacker as an Irishman acting without provocation despite the fact that Sprague, the only witness, had not yet been able to provide any information. The boy later recovered sufficiently enough to offer an account of the incident, which included no mention of his attacker being Irish.

Dorr's guilty verdict of May 7, 1844, and his sentence of imprisonment for a life of hard labor, did little to quell their emotions.

Despite being confined to the same state prison that they shared with Dorr, John and Nicholas Gordon were not allowed to see each other, nor were they allowed any contact with their family. The separation ended on October 9, 1844, however, when the supreme court finally heard arguments on John's motion for a new trial. In record time, Justice Durfee, emphasizing the brutality of the murder and the impartiality of the trial, promptly rejected the defense arguments and denied the petition. John Gordon was sentenced to be hanged

Early portrait of
Thomas Wilson Dorr.
*Courtesy of the Rhode
Island State Library.*

in the yard of the state prison on February 14, 1845. Looking at John Gordon, Durfee asked, "Why should the sentence of death not be passed upon you?" Numb to the court ruling, Gordon stood tall and replied, "Gentlemen, these may be my last words, I therefore here declare, that I never had hand, act or part in the murder of Mr. Sprague. I never had hand, act or part in the murder of any man, woman or child. I further declare, that I never knew that gentleman. My prosecutors have wickedly and maliciously sworn away my life, and it is always more easy to do to a stranger, than towards one who is well known. I have no more than this to say."

Gordon's lack of remorse clearly irritated the judge.

Chapter 28

THE TRIAL OF NICHOLAS GORDON:
OCTOBER 19–OCTOBER 31

"It Resembles the Gun I Saw John Have,
in Its General Appearance"

Four days later, on October 19, the trial of Nicholas Gordon began. While the court and the prosecution remained unchanged from John's trial, the defense team was different. Samuel Atwell, who now lay close to death, was absent, and Samuel Currey replaced Thomas Carpenter. Currey was very much a part of the Rhode Island establishment. He was every bit as conservative as the prosecutors and consequently conducted a more aggressive and effective defense than Atwell and Carpenter had in the trial of Nicholas's brothers.

As the defense had expected, the facts testified to by the witnesses in this trial, although from the same witnesses, were dramatically different. Abner Sprague Jr., for example, was certain during John and William Gordon's trial that the gun he had seen John Gordon carry just two days before the murder was the exact weapon found at the crime scene. Yet in this trial he could say only that "it *resemble[d]* the gun I saw John have, in its general appearance [emphasis added]." Likewise, Charles Searle and Richard Knight each had a different version of events that took place at the council meeting at which Nicholas's liquor license was denied. At John's trial, Searle testified that Amasa Sprague was present at the July 1843 meeting and had personally opposed the granting of Nicholas's license, which the council roundly rejected. At this trial, however, he testified that Sprague was ill and had not attended the July meeting although he did attend the August meeting and opposed the license renewal at that time. While this seems like a relatively insignificant and innocent mix-up in dates at first glance, the new testimony actually meant that Nicholas Gordon could not have sent for his brothers from Ireland for the purpose of seeking revenge, as was alleged in the first trial, because he had sent for his entire family—and they had arrived—prior to the August meeting. This new testimony caused severe damage to the prosecution's allegations of motive and conspiracy on which John Gordon's conviction was hinged and might have served John Gordon well had he been granted a new trial or if his sentencing had been delayed until after the second trial. Richard Knight corroborated Searle's testimony.

Susan Field, the prostitute who had originally testified that she visited Nicholas Gordon's store as many as three times per week, now admitted that she "was not living in Cranston [for much of the time in question] but in North Providence, several miles distant" and lived in Cranston with her mother only from May through July 1843.

The defense witnesses testified that they never heard Nicholas Gordon make threats against Sprague and were more matter of fact about the council's denial of the liquor license renewal. Another testified that any threats he heard were against the council, not against Sprague. Still others said that Gordon blamed his fellow Irishmen for the loss of his license because of their signatures on the remonstrance submitted to the council.

After eight days and one hundred witnesses, the trial was over. In his jury instructions, Judge Durfee made no mention of William's acquittal but noted that the jury must consider whether Nicholas incited John to commit the murder on his behalf. Unlike those in the trial of John Gordon, the jurors in Nicholas's trial agonized for sixteen hours before advising the court that they were hopelessly deadlocked with eight members voting for conviction and four for acquittal. The jury was dismissed, and a new trial was ordered.

Four days later, Samuel Atwell, the courageous attorney who took up the cause of righteousness, lost his battle for life. While he lived long enough to learn of the result of Nicholas's trial, he would never know the fate of John Gordon—at least not in this world.

Chapter 29

THE EXECUTION OF JOHN GORDON

"I Do. I Forgive All My Enemies, and Persecutors. I Forgive Them for They Know Not What They Do"

E very attempt by the defense to postpone what now appeared inevitable had failed. The court denied the 1844 motion for a new trial. A January 1845 petition to the court and two simultaneous petitions to the general assembly, each signed by numerous members of the public including clergymen, requesting postponement of John Gordon's execution pending the outcome of Nicholas's trial were also denied. The house petition was rejected on a narrow vote of twenty-seven in favor and thirty-six against, meaning a shift of just five votes would have provided the requested delay of execution.

A senate resolution taken up just four days later would have created a joint committee to consider a suspension of John Gordon's sentence. The vote failed by a larger margin, perhaps as a result of a polarizing debate on a bill to grant amnesty to Thomas Dorr that was held in the days between the votes on the two Gordon bills.

Adding to John Gordon's misfortune is the fact that William's disclosure of hiding the guns that belonged to Nicholas—certain proof that neither of those guns could have served as the murder weapon—did not come until the eighth day after the legislative votes were taken. The possibility exists that William's secret may have been sufficient to change the mind of at least five legislators. Neither William nor history ever explained why he waited so long to reveal his agonizing secret. It is surmised, though, that he was simply too afraid or too ashamed to reveal the details of what he had done, believing that his own actions cost John his life.

James Fenner served as governor of Rhode Island from 1807 to 1811, 1824 to 1831 and again from 1843 to 1845. He was serving in office when the petition to delay John Gordon's execution until after the trial of Nicholas Gordon was presented for consideration. He denied the petition, allowing the execution to take place as scheduled. *State House Portrait Collection.*

At mid-day on February 10, 1845, with time running out for John, Attorney John Knowles petitioned Governor James Fenner one last time, begging that the execution be delayed until after the second trial of Nicholas. Knowles wrote:

> *A friend has within the hour informed me that he has good reason to believe that the Judges of the Supreme Court are unanimously of opinion that John Gordon ought, as a matter of right, to be reprieved, until after a second trial of his brother Nicholas, for on his trial, Nicholas assumes on himself the burden of proving the innocence of John. He assumed this on his late trial, and as a juror, Mr. Mathewson, informs me, the Jury disagreed upon John's case, rather than upon that of Nicholas.*

John Gordon himself, in a petition prepared by his attorney and presented to Governor Fenner, disclosed new details that might support the call for a postponement of the execution until after the second trial of Nicholas. The petition read:

To His Excellency James Fenner, Governor of the State of Rhode Island

The undersigned, John Gordon, a convict under the sentence of death humbly asks from your Excellency an examination of the accompanying affidavits; and in view of their contents, and of the circumstances under which he was convicted (too familiar to all to be here recited), invokes such action on your part as to your Excellency shall seem meet.

He is sentenced to be executed on Friday next, the 14th instant, between the hours of nine and three. The facts set forth in the affidavit of William Gordon, considered in connexion [sic] with the testimony upon which your petitioner was convicted—facts withheld by the petitioner, even from his counsel, lest by a disclosure he should jeopard [sic] his brother William, and never divulged to Counsel until Saturday last—these facts, your petitioner submits, entitle him to ask a reprieved until his brother Nicholas shall have been again tried.

Wherefore he would now, as a citizen preferring a not unreasonable petition to the Executive Power, ask from your Excellency, (if constitutionally it may be) a reprieve "until the end of the next session of the Assembly;" or such other proper executive action, as shall afford him an opportunity to solicit from the Legislature of the State a consideration of his case, and that reprieve, which recently (for want of that which is herewith presented) was denied him.

And as in duty bound, will pray.

John Gordon

Accompanying the above letter was an affidavit of William Gordon that declared that following the arrests of Nicholas and John, he entered Nicholas's store and saw the gun standing in the corner of the room on the right of the door. William explains:

It instantly occurred to me that as John and Nicholas had been arrested, the house would be searched to find weapons, and that as in my own country, where few persons, comparatively, of the poorer classes possess arms, the finding of weapons in the house of the suspected is almost enough to insure a conviction, it would be greatly to my brothers' advantage to conceal the gun. I then...instantly returned to the kitchen door, which I had left partly open, and closed it; and then taking the gun went up-stairs with it into the garret. Then turning to the left, I tore up the cloth carpeting between the two beds which stood there, and tried to loosen one of the floor boards with my fingers. Failing this, I looked around for some implement to aid

> me, and after a few minutes' search found a crooked piece of iron, with
> which I forced up the end of one of the floorboards and thrust the gun
> in as far as it would go. The gun was not yet wholly out of sight, and I
> therefore attempted to raise the next board. In doing this I split the board,
> but accomplished my purpose, as I was then able to put the gun out of
> sight…The next morning…I found lying upon the upper shelf a small
> pocket pistol, which I knew to be Nicholas', as I had often seen it in his
> possession. This I immediately took up, and for the same reason which had
> actuated me in concealing the gun proceeded forthwith to secrete. I went
> upstairs with it, and on looking for a fit hiding place, noticed the hole in
> the floor through which the stovepipe from the shop passed. I perceived that
> between the joists under the garret floor was a cavity, and into that I put the
> pistol, pushing it in as far as I could with a stick about a yard long.

The affidavit goes on to say that right after doing that he went to the jail
to inform Nicholas and John of his "proceedings in relation to the gun and
the pistol; but on reaching the jail was denied access to them and thereupon
set off for home," where he was arrested about a hundred yards shy of
Sprague's house. In jail he was further denied access to his brothers. William
further acknowledges that he never had the opportunity to relay this story
to Nicholas but told John only during their trial while the two sat together
in the courtroom:

> A few days after my acquittal, availing myself of the temporary absence
> from the home of my mother and sister, I took the gun from its hiding place
> and drew the charge. It was loaded with powder and shot. I then put it
> back in the cavity, and there it remained undisturbed, until last fall, when
> I exhibited it to a Mr. Mathewson and a Mr. Chapman, as will appear
> hereafter. Shortly after this I drew the pistol out of the place where I had
> put it, and laid it in Nicholas' trunk down stairs, where it remained unseen
> so far as I know, until within a few days, when I showed it to Mr. John
> Devlin, of Pawtucket.

Despite the overwhelming evidence revealed in the affidavits in support
of a reprieve, and despite the affirmation of those mentioned as having
seen the weapons described by William, Governor James Fenner, after
reviewing the petition, opined in a written response dated February 10,
1845, that section four, article seven of the Rhode Island constitution gives
him the power to "grant a reprieve after conviction, in all cases except

those of impeachment, until the end of the next session of the General Assembly," thus limiting the exercise of the power to a specific term. Because there had been four sessions since the sentencing, Fenner was constitutionally restricted from taking the requested action. Apparently, justice was not worth any deviation from one's perceived authority, even if that action in the pursuit of justice would not alter, in any way, the state's ability to carry through with the sentence it had imposed.

The general assembly did manage enough votes, however, to prevent John and Nicholas from seeing each other before John's execution. In fact, the assembly ordered that the brothers be housed in separate cells so distant from each other that communication between the two was impossible.

Despite overwhelming evidence of his innocence, John Gordon was out of options. More importantly, he was out of time. He didn't spend his last three days on earth lamenting the decisions by the court, the general assembly or the governor, however. Nor did he curse his detractors. Rather, he pragmatically approached his own demise. He expressed his forgiveness of William, who visited John every day until the last.

At about ten o'clock in the morning of February 14, 1845, prison guards escorted John's brother William and Father John Brady, the parish priest from the Church of Saints Peter and Paul, into John's cell. John was pale and haggard, the result of months of anguish and incarceration with felons. The three men talked and prayed in John's cell for about an hour, what surely seemed the quickest hour since his incarceration so many months ago. At eleven o'clock the sheriff entered the cell and, appearing visually affected, adjusted John's white robe and cap. As they took what would be John's final walk, he was calm and composed as if nothing was about to transpire.

In the corridor, John met his brother Nicholas, whom he had not seen for almost a year. The two embraced in a long farewell, at which time John urged Nicholas to take courage and not be downhearted. They soon parted company, and John left the confines of the cold, damp and impersonal prison walls for the last time. As he walked through the steel door and into the biting, wintery chill of the prison yard, he gazed at those assembled to witness his demise. The sheriff and Father Brady accompanied John up the stairs of the scaffold that had been constructed in the prison yard.

Here, in plain view of the sixty witnesses allowed to attend the execution, the prisoner was expected to confess his guilt. It was customary in such settings for the guilty man to ask—no—to beg the forgiveness of God and his fellow man. But today's events would not follow the customary script. Neither did Father Brady's final words to the condemned man "follow the

This 1845 sketch shows the Rhode Island State Prison in the old cove, the site of modern-day Providence Place Mall. This is the prison that housed the John and William Gordon and Thomas Dorr. John Gordon was hanged on this site outside the walls of the prison. *From* Brotherly Love *by Charles and Tess Hoffmann.*

Providence fo. Feby 14th 1845

I hereby Certify that I have this day at Eleven O Clock A.M. Received the body of John Gordon from the Jailor of the Providence County Jail and Executed him according to sentence

Roger Williams Potter Shff

The February 14, 1845 execution report of John Gordon whereby Sheriff Roger Potter notes receipt of Gordon's body at 11:00 a.m. *Courtesy of the Rhode Island State Archives.*

expected ritual of platitudinous spiritual solace for a remorseful or guilty criminal." Father Brady said simply, "Have courage, John; you are going to appear before a just and merciful Judge. You are going to join myriads of your countrymen, who, like you, were sacrificed at the shrine of bigotry and prejudice. Forgive your enemies."

Gordon looked longingly at his priest and responded, "I do. I forgive all my enemies, and persecutors. I forgive them for they know not what they do." He looked to the crowd assembled and said, "I hope all good Christians will pray for me." Then Gordon faced the sheriff and with a nod of his head said, "Yes, I'm ready."

A handkerchief that was given to John by his mother was used to cover his eyes. It was tied around his head and the noose fixed tightly on his neck. As he stepped onto the trapdoor, he seemed to falter. Within seconds, anti-gallows judge William Staples pulled the lever releasing the platform beneath John's feet. The fall and sudden stop as the rope reached its limit snapped John's neck. His body jerked from side to side as the last vestige of life left his dangling body. Death was almost instantaneous. Yet, as if in retribution for his perceived lack of remorse and his failure to admit guilt, John's body was left hanging on the gallows for twenty minutes. When finally removed from beneath the scaffold, John's limp body was placed in a coffin that was simply inscribed, "John Gordon, Aged 29 years."

A large group of his countrymen that waited on the outside of the prison walls accompanied the coffin past the house of Amasa Sprague and to the home of Nicholas Gordon. His funeral took place two days later on Sunday, February 16. Despite the ardent belief in his innocence, and the disdain for those who refused to delay the execution beyond the date of Nicholas's second trial, there were no demonstrations or outbursts by the mourners or protesters during the funeral. The procession of some 1,400 Irishmen was quiet, orderly and impressive. Mourners included friends and countrymen, of course, but also Irishmen and sympathizers from as far away as Connecticut and Massachusetts, who were present to make a political statement.

They followed a circuitous route to the North Burial Ground. Mourners followed the coffin across the Crawford Street Bridge in Providence, bypassing the direct route to North Main Street and instead choosing to go up the hill to Benefit Street, where they marched for about a mile. They carried John's coffin past the statehouse where the Rhode Island judicial system had failed to carry out his promised and expected justice. The procession continued past the house of Sullivan Dorr where Thomas Dorr had been raised. And, in a final tribute to the miscarriage of justice, John's body was taken past the house of Susan Field, the prostitute whose perjury helped convict him. They finally arrived at the North Burial Ground where the body of John Gordon was laid to rest in a pauper's grave provided by the government. Later, friends would relocate his coffin to an unmarked grave in the cemetery of Saint Mary's in Pawtucket so as to commit John's body to the eternal sanctuary of hallowed ground.

Chapter 30

THE SECOND TRIAL OF NICHOLAS GORDON

"Thank God I Didn't Kill Him. I Wasn't There"

On the morning of Monday, April 7, 1845, the second trial of Nicholas Gordon began. John Gordon's execution was being widely denounced as the murder of an innocent man, and the Dorrites had experienced unbridled success at the polls. Yet, perhaps hoping to prove that they had not erred in the case of John Gordon, the government did not back down in its efforts to continue the charade. A new government witness who testified that he heard Nicholas say, "Amasa Sprague, God damn him, has prevented me from getting a license, and before another year, I'll be revenged on him, or I'll pay him for it," was forced to admit on cross-examination that he "thought it at the time to be bar-room talk." The gun evidence was cast into doubt when Augustus Moffit, on cross-examination, said, referring to the murder weapon, "The bore of the gun Nicholas had was larger than the one in court." Even the final prosecution witness contradicted earlier testimony when, under oath, he quoted Nicholas Gordon as saying, "Thank God I didn't kill him. I wasn't there." He also testified that Nicholas expressed sympathy for Sprague's death.

After days of testimony from tens of witnesses, the jury reported at 10:30 a.m. on April 17 that they were hopelessly deadlocked with nine voting for acquittal and only three for conviction. Despite the two hung juries and the fact that the state had no apparent intention of bringing a new trial, Attorney General Blake opposed bail for Nicholas Gordon.

Ironically enough, Charles Jackson, the newly elected governor, promoted the release of Thomas Dorr on the same day that Nicholas Gordon's second trial began. Durfee ruled that Gordon would be held pending payment of the sizeable sum of $10,000 in bail. The surety was paid by several prominent residents, and on April 18, 1845, Nicholas Gordon was released from prison after being incarcerated for some fifteen months. Though out of prison, Gordon was not a free man because the charges were not dropped, leaving the ever-present threat of a new trial hanging over his head.

Eighteen months later, on October 22, 1846, Nicholas Gordon died, leaving behind significant debt for which his brother William was arrested and incarcerated on June 18, 1850. Ellen Gordon was also at risk of incarceration for the same indebtedness, but she was not arrested. There seemed little point. Her life, which had so much promise when Nicholas paid her way to America, was now a shambles. Two of her sons were dead, and William was in prison.

William Gordon's life was shattered. Never able to shake from his consciousness the words his brother John whispered to him on his conviction, William was wracked with guilt. That sense of responsibility for John's execution, coupled with his own legal concerns, caused him to drink intemperately. In 1851, William was released from prison and admitted to Dexter Asylum. The asylum "served as an institution for the care of the poor, aged and mentally ill of Providence from 1829 to 1957." William, while under the care of the asylum doctors, was forced to work on the asylum's farm. William, as did most patients, clearly disliked conditions at Dexter, and on March 26, 1852, he deserted. He lived with his mother at 17 Pond Street in Providence. Though William was drunk more than sober, she provided his care as best she could, but by 1857, she could no longer handle his drunkenness. William was readmitted to Dexter on November 14 and remained for 164 days. He was released on April 26, 1858, on intemperate discharge. This pattern repeated itself later in 1858 and again in 1860, with each occurrence requiring longer stays and each discharge taking place against doctor's recommendations. The asylum's doctors noted the severity of William's case and his declining condition in the official records but were powerless to prevent his mother from forcing his release—that is, until his final admission on October 6, 1862. This time, not even Ellen could help William, who died at the asylum on May 8, 1862, after 204 days of confinement.

For her part, Ellen was able to escape the confines of a prison cell, but was by no means free. She faced the ever-present threat of imprisonment for Nicholas's debt and the intense pain of a once-proud family now as shattered as her very image of the American dream. She was unable to support herself, and her family name had been ruined. The house she had purchased from Nicholas for $1.00 was sold at public auction for $1.20 in taxes owed on January 5, 1852, forcing her to rent the small apartment at 17 Pond Street in Providence where she lived until her own commitment to the Dexter Asylum on June 26, 1862, just a little over a month after the death of her third son, William. There she lived out her remaining days. Ellen died of kidney disease on September 7, 1862 at the age of seventy.

The youngest brother, Robert, had married a Nova Scotia woman by the name of Sarah some years earlier and lived at 20 Cargill Street in Providence, just a short distance from his mother's apartment. The couple had seven children, one of which died very young.

Margaret Gordon married John O'Hearn on May 7, 1847 at St. Patrick's Church. Father W. Wiley officiated at the ceremony, but lacking the presence of her older brothers, the day was not as joyful an occasion as it ought to have been. She most likely thought about them, as did her mother, but struggled to redirect her attention to happier thoughts. The couple also made their home in Providence.

The building belonging to Nicholas, and then Ellen—the house of death as it was once called—was destroyed sometime around 1930, and the land on which it sat is now ironically, if not appropriately, part of Saint Ann's Catholic cemetery.

If anything good resulted from one of Rhode Island's darkest judicial moments, it might be that the imbalance in the scales of justice experienced by John Gordon, and the subsequent destruction of nearly the entire Gordon family, led to the abolition of the state's death penalty.

Public sentiment against the death penalty had been on the rise even before John Gordon's execution. In 1838, the general assembly issued a report recommending revisions to the penal code that would abolish the death penalty. Since 1673, there had been a total of fifty-two executions in Rhode Island (forty-five as a colony and seven as a state), but now the assembly leaders believed that John Gordon's should be the last. On January 23, 1852, after seven years of discussion and debate regarding the Gordon case, the senate committee on education issued a report on the history and merits of capital punishment. The resulting vote by the full assembly, led by the Democratic supporters of Thomas Wilson Dorr, taken on February 11, 1852, abolished capital punishment in Rhode Island in its entirety. In 1872, a new law was passed reinstating the death penalty only in the case of murder committed by someone serving a life sentence. No one was ever put to death under this law. On June 26, 1973, the Rhode Island general assembly passed legislation providing for the death penalty by lethal gas for murders committed by persons while under confinement at the state correctional facilities. Although four men were awaiting execution under this act, the Rhode Island Supreme Court ruled the law unconstitutional in 1979. On May 9, 1984, the general assembly enacted Public Law Chapter 221 removing the mandatory death sentence language from Rhode Island General Law 11-23-2.

John Gordon remains the last man ever executed in the state of Rhode Island. His courage and ability to forgive his aggressors as encouraged by his Catholic faith, even under the most extreme bigoted and inequitable of circumstances, might just prove to be his greatest legacy.

Chapter 31

THE PARDON OF JOHN GORDON

"Forgiveness Is the Ultimate Revenge"

Rhode Island state representative Peter Martin was at his home in Newport when he received a call from Ancient Order of Hibernians State President Rick O'Neill, asking if he would be interested in meeting with local playwright Ken Dooley. A native of Cranston, Rhode Island, Dooley had just completed work on his play *The Murder Trial of John Gordon*, which was going to debut at the newly renovated, historic Park Theater in Cranston. Dooley, who recalls his grandmother singing "a little ditty about Poor Johnny Gordon," wrote the play detailing the events surrounding the biased trial and wrongful execution of an Irish Catholic immigrant, John Gordon, back in the mid-nineteenth century. "As far as I'm concerned, they murdered that kid," Dooley said.

Martin agreed to meet with Dooley and was provided a sound introduction to the incredible details of John Gordon's case. Martin sought advice from his former Rhode Island House of Representatives colleague Attorney General Peter F. Kilmartin. Kilmartin's simple response was that "justice has no statute of limitations." It didn't take Martin too long to realize what he needed to do. He met Governor Lincoln Chafee, a man of old Yankee stock himself, in the hallway at the statehouse and briefly explained to the governor his interest in obtaining a posthumous pardon of John Gordon for the murder of Cranston industrialist Amasa Sprague. Governor Chafee's immediate response was, "I know that case; we must help that man!"

Out of respect for the law and proper procedure, Representative Martin wanted to have the "full facts of the case" reviewed by the general assembly.

In 2010, playwright Ken Dooley presented *The Murder Trial of John Gordon*. The play served as a launching pad for legislation introduced by Representative Peter Martin of Newport to pardon John Gordon for the murder of Amasa Sprague. *From the author's collection.*

As soon as he had introduced the resolution, Michael DiLauro, an assistant public defender, who, as a history buff had long been fascinated with the Gordon case, approached Martin. DiLauro told Representative Martin of his long interest in, and extensive knowledge of, the John Gordon case. He explained that the case led to the abolition of the death penalty in Rhode Island. With the encouragement of public defender John Hardiman, he offered to act as the defense attorney in any hearings on the matter.

The bill also drew the support of the Catholic Church. Father Bernard Healey, the legislative liaison for the Diocese of Providence, took an active part in the legislative proceedings. "John Gordon was put to death because he was Catholic," Father Healey told lawmakers. "It was Catholics in the nineteenth century. Who will it be this century?"

A house judiciary committee hearing was held to review the resolution. Testimony was provided by Ken Dooley, Michael DiLauro and Father Healey, as well as noted Rhode Island historians Scott Molloy and Patrick Conley and the much-respected director of the local American Civil Liberties Union, Steven Brown. Martin told his colleagues: "This was an injustice done by the state of Rhode Island by our predecessors. We have many responsibilities to the citizens of Rhode Island. Justice is one of them, isn't it?"

After gaining unanimous support in the committee, the resolution passed in the house of representatives by a vote of seventy to zero. Representative Michael Chippendale viewed his support of the measure as an opportunity to teach children "that intolerance will always end in injustice."

The measure was sent to the senate where DiLauro submitted an amicus brief on behalf of the bill. The full senate supported the resolution on a vote of thirty-three to three. "To me," said Senator Harold Metts, a clergyman of Cape Verdean descent, "it's a matter of healing. They called it an execution…we called it a lynching."

Both the house and senate resolutions made their way to the desk of Governor Lincoln Chafee, who was an ardent opponent of capital punishment. DiLauro submitted a revised copy of his amicus brief to the governor, who was clearly in support of the action.

In an impressive ceremony, he officially pardoned John Gordon on June 29, 2011. The governor had his own connection to the saga as his great-great-uncle, Zechariah Chafee, had been named a bankruptcy trustee of the Sprague estate after the 1870s collapse of the Sprague Manufacturing Company. Zechariah Chafee then became entangled in a legal dispute over the amount of his payment and the company's assets.

On June 29, 2011, a ceremony was held to formally pardon John Gordon. In this photo, Governor Lincoln Chafee reads the Declaration of Pardon prior to the signing. *Courtesy of the Rhode Island General Assembly.*

Governor Chafee (seated) hands the pen he just used to sign the pardon to Representative Peter F. Martin, the sponsor of the house resolution and a prime mover in the effort to pardon John Gordon. Looking on are (from left to right) Senator Michael J. McCaffrey, the sponsor of the senate resolution, House Speaker Gordon D. Fox and Senator Erin P. Lynch. *Courtesy of the Rhode Island House of Representatives.*

Governor Lincoln Chafee (center) holds the signed copy of the pardon of John Gordon during the June 29 ceremony. The pardoning took place in the same courtroom in which Gordon was convicted and sentenced to death 166 years earlier. The governor is flanked by historian Scott Malloy (left) and Representative Peter F. Martin (right), who was instrumental in the success of the movement to pardon Gordon. *Photo courtesy of the Rhode Island House of Representatives.*

Lincoln Chafee signed the proclamation of pardon at the Old State House on Benefit Street, the same courtroom where Gordon's trial had taken place 166 years earlier. He acknowledged that "Gordon had been put to death after a highly questionable judicial process and based on no concrete evidence. There was no question he was not given a fair trial. Today we are trying to right that injustice." The very room where John Gordon was once sentenced to death was now full of supporters who applauded Gordon's long-denied justice.

Finally an exonerated man, John Gordon was provided a proper headstone at his burial place at Saint Mary's Cemetery in Pawtucket despite his body remaining in an unmarked grave in the same cemetery. The dedication ceremony took place on Saturday, October 8, 2011, with a noontime remembrance that was attended by about fifty people including legislators, priests and members of the Pawtucket Chapter of the Friendly Sons of Saint Patrick, among them Shaun O'Brien, who organized the service.

Above: Close-up of the plaque on the grave of John Gordon. *Photo by the author, 2012.*

Opposite: The monument of John Gordon at Saint Mary's Cemetery in Pawtucket, Rhode Island. *Photo by the author, 2012.*

The ceremony began with a Mass of remembrance at Saint Mary's Church. Former house speaker Matthew J. Smith, an Irish Catholic historian, and one of Gordon's earliest modern defenders, provided a stirring eulogy. Doctor Scott Malloy, who had been teaching the Gordon case for about twenty-five years, and Rhode Island Historian Laureate Dr. Patrick T. Conley were the principal speakers. Dublin-born Tom Lanigan, a local songwriter and musician, sang a special song that he wrote for the occasion called "The Ballad of John Gordon." The song has since been released on CD, on which Representative Martin plays the harmonica.

Ken Dooley recently completed the screenplay of John Gordon's story that is now under consideration by several Hollywood producers for a full-length motion picture. But it was the final line from Dooley's play that provided the epitaph on the headstone that stands at the entrance to the original 1829 church (the oldest surviving Catholic church in Rhode Island). The inscription reads simply: "Forgiveness is the ultimate revenge."

Chapter 32

THE HAUNTING OF SPRAGUESVILLE

"Tell My Story"

The 1790 Cranston Street mansion that was once home to the socially and politically powerful Sprague family had seen its share of cursed happenings: the murder of Amasa Sprague on New Year's Eve 1843, a hanging suicide that took place in the hallway off the stairwell, the unearthing of several household servants buried in the backyard without benefit of coffin or headstone and, perhaps most egregious, the travesty of justice that resulted in the wrongful hanging of a man whose noose was tightened by the unfair judicial wrangling of prejudice and insincerity. Sprague's actual murderer was never found.

It was 1968, and a student from Brown University who lived in the grand old Sprague house as a caretaker had invited some of his friends to help him locate the spirits that had molested him during his stay. The student had been aware of the many rumors of hauntings and apparitions before he agreed to move in, and he had experienced, firsthand, some of the home's strange episodes after his arrival. The student and his friends sat around the table, six or seven of them, but none was ready for what was about to happen. The flame from the candle in the center of the table provided the only flicker of light in the otherwise darkened room. Joining hands, one of the participants cried out, "If you are the one disturbing the peace of this house reveal yourself." From the beyond they received an answer that no one, not even those participating the séance, really expected.

Those holding hands at the table tightened their grip. "What do you need to be at peace?" the student asked. "Tell my story," the Ouija board

This fragment of Amasa Sprague's original gravestone was unearthed in the rear yard of the Sprague mansion when the area was being excavated for the construction of neighborhood homes. Sprague's body was initially laid to rest on the mansion property but was later moved to the Swan Point Cemetery in Providence. *Photo by the author, 2012.*

The Sprague Mansion at 1351 Cranston Street, Cranston, Rhode Island. *Photo by the author, 2012.*

The interior hallway of the Sprague mansion where one of the Sprague relatives hanged himself in the years following Amasa's murder. *Photo by the author, 2012.*

spelled out. Then fear filled the eyes of all those seated when inexplicably the Ouija board being used as a means of contacting the spirits began to repeatedly and violently spell out the words "MY LAND!" That brought a quick end to the séance. The frightened group disbanded and seldom spoke of the experience.

Supernatural disturbances had taken place at this birthplace of two Rhode Island governors since 1925, when the first apparitions of a man walking down the stairwell between the first and second floor were reported. The wine cellar too had its share of supernatural phenomena, including the feeling of cold winds, apparitions of Amasa Sprague and the passing breath of icy air. In the upstairs bedrooms, blankets have been pulled off beds while unsuspecting guests slept in them. Footsteps are sometimes heard coming from the Doll Room, so named because of the large number of dolls that adorn the walls, and dolls have mysteriously moved about. Other visitors report lights turning on and off by themselves. Still others complain of feeling an unearthly presence when they are alone in the room.

The Sprague mansion at 1351 Cranston Street in Cranston, Rhode Island, which has been described as one of the most haunted mansions in America, was also host to the producers of the popular SciFi network show *Ghost Hunters* who disclosed strange occurrences. Those bizarre happenings continue to this day.

The Cranston Historical Society provides tours by appointment, and while one may experience some of the supernatural phenomena at any time, the best chance of seeing the spirit of Amasa Sprague is reportedly around the anniversary of his death in December.

Whether or not ghosts actually roam the halls of the Sprague mansion is a matter of debate. In a sense, however, the city of Cranston—indeed the entire state of Rhode Island—will forever be haunted by the memories of the hatred, prejudice and bias that destroyed the hopes and dreams of one Irish Catholic family and the innocence of an entire generation of Irish Catholic immigrants that lived here. The stain of that injustice may well haunt us forever.

BIBLIOGRAPHY

BOOKS

Barry, John M. *Roger Williams and the Creation of the American Soul.* New York: Viking, 2012.

Conley, Patrick T. *An Album of Rhode Island History, 1636–1986.* East Providence, RI: Rhode Island Publications Society, 1992.

———. *Liberty and Justice: A History of Law and Lawyers in Rhode Island, 1636–1998.* East Providence, RI: Rhode Island Publications Society, 1998.

———. *People, Places, Laws and Lore of the Ocean State: A Rhode Island Historical Sampler.* East Providence, RI: Rhode Island Publications Society, 2012.

Conley, Patrick T., and Matthew J. Smith. *Catholicism in Rhode Island: The Formative Era.* Providence, RI: Diocese of Providence, 1976.

Gaustad, Edwin S. *Liberty of Conscience: Roger Williams in America.* Valley Forge, PA: Judson Press, 1999.

Geake, Robert A. *Historic Taverns of Rhode Island.* Charleston, SC: The History Press, 2012.

Gettleman, Marvin E. *The Dorr Rebellion: A Study in American Radicalism 1833–1849,* New York: Random House, 1973.

Glocester Bicentennial Commission. *Glocester: The Way Up Country: A History, Guide and Directory.* Glocester, RI: Town of Glocester, 1976.

Hoffman, Charles, and Tess Hoffman. *Brotherly Love.* Amherst: University of Massachusetts Press, 1993.

Kellner, George H., and J. Stanley Lemons. *Rhode Island: The Independent State,* Windsor Publications, 1982.

Larned, Edward C., and William Knowles. *The Trial of John and William Gordon Charged with the Murder of Amasa Sprague, Before the Supreme Court of Rhode Island, March Term, 1844.* Providence, RI: Sydney S. Ryder, 1884.

Rapoza, Lydia L., and Bette Miller. *Cranston*. Charleston, SC: Arcadia Publishing, 1999.

Raven, Rory. *The Dorr War: Treason, Rebellion and the Fight for Reform in Rhode Island.* Charleston, SC: The History Press, 2010.

State of Rhode Island. *Memorial of Henry Bowen Anthony*. Providence: Rhode Island General Assembly, 1885.

Interviews by the Author

DeLauro, Michael, public defender and historian that provided an amicus brief to the general assembly and governor in support of the Gordon pardon. In discussion with author. State House, Providence, RI. January 3, 2013.

Dooley, Ken, playwright and author, *The Murder of John Gordon*. In discussion with author. Newport, RI. January 23, 2013.

Hall, James, curator of the Sprague Mansion. In discussion with the author. Cranston, RI. December 28, 2012.

Martin, Peter, state representative from Newport that introduced the resolution to pardon John Gordon. In discussion with the author. January 3 and 23, 2013.

Internet Sources

Camarda, Nicole. "Murder at the Sprague Mansion." *Rhode Island Roads*, May 17, 2005. www.riroads.com.

Condit, Jon. "The Apparition. October 14, 2007." www.dreadcentral.com/story.

"Death of an Irishman." *A Silver Voice From Ireland*, June 28, 2011. www.thesilvervoice. wordpress.com.

Duffy, Charles F. Honest. *Hardworking, But Shiftless: Henry David Thoreau on Irish Immigrants*. www.kouroo.info/thoreau/thoreauO.

"1845: John Gordon, the Last Hanged in Rhode Island." *Executed Today*, February 14, 2012. www.executedtoday.com.

Historic Locations, The Spragues and Sprague Mansion. www.cranstonri.com/generalpage.php?.

Historical Summary: Ireland in the first decade of the 1800s–1830s. www.1.xe.net.

"Irishman Officially Pardoned 166 Years After His Execution." *The Journal*, August 9, 2011. www.thejournal.ie.

"Notable Rhode Island Execution." *Crime and Punishment Forum*, January 17, 2011. www.cncpunishment.com Pasco, Eva. "Tour Cranston, RI's Sprague Mansion—

Homestead Haunted by a Travesty of Justice." www.exinearticles.com/?Tour-Cranston-Sprague-Mansion.

"Rhode Island Inequity." *Murder by Gaslight*, July 17, 2010. www.murderbygaslight.blogspot.com.

www.cathedralprovidence.org—Information regarding the history of Saints Peter and Paul Church.

www.cranstonhistoricalsociety.org—The Governor Sprague Mansion.

www.freerepublic.com/focus/f-re—In 150 Year Old Case, Rhode Island Confronts Anti-Catholic Past.

www.gentlemensemporium.com—Information regarding the style of dress in the 1840s.

www.historicalcemeteries.ri.gov—Rhode Island Historical Cemetery Commission website.

www.its.ilstu.edu/cjhistory/amasa.htm—Looks at the Sprague murder case from a legalistic point of view.

www.myilsto.edu/-ftmorn/cjhistory—The Murder of Amasa Sprague.

www.reocities.com/CollegePark/Quad/6460/dir/845nativ.html—Offers information about nativism in the United States in the nineteenth century.

www.reocities.com—The Verdict and Beyond.

www.sprague-database.org—Traces the history of the Sprague Family. Developed by Richard E. Weber. Albert Arnold Sprague, IV, Webmaster.

www.spraguemansion.com—The official website of the Sprague mansion owned by the Cranston Historical Society.

www.stacyhouse.com—Website of state Representative Peter Martin.

www.wikipedia.org—Cathedral of Saints Peter and Paul, Providence, History.

www.wikipedia.org—Providence, Rhode Island, Geography.

www.wikipedia.org/wiki/knightsville—History of Knightsville.

www.wikipedia.org/wiki/providence—Historical information on the city of Providence.

www.youtube.com—Rhode Island Catholic. Memorial to an Irish Immigrant.

PERIODICALS

Acts and Resolves passed by the General Assembly of the State of Rhode Island and Providence Plantations at the January Session, A.D. 1956. Oxford Press, 1956.

Brayton, Gladys W. "Who Killed Amasa Sprague?" *Old Stone Bank.*

Butman, Dean P. "His Murder Changed Rhode Island Law." *Rhode Island Yearbook, 1968* (1968): 108–14.

"The chain of circumstantial evidence…" *Providence Journal*, January 3, 1844.

DiLauro, Michael A. "Rhode Island Public Defender amicus brief in support of the House and Senate Resolutions requesting a gubernatorial pardon of John Gordon." Providence, 2011.

Dooley, Ken. *The Murder Trial of John Gordon*. Playbill. Rhode Island Center For Performing Arts. January 14–February 7, 2011.

"Examination of the Gordons." *Providence Journal*, January 16, 1844.

Fraga, Brian. "Production Portrays Persecuted Catholic in New Light." *Rhode Island Catholic*, Jaunary 6, 2011.

———. "Rewriting History Clearing John Gordon's Name After 166 Years." *Rhode Island Catholic*, May 19, 2011.

Gray, Channing. "Murder, Immigrants and R.I. Politics." *Providence Journal*, January 2011.

———. "Well-Told—If a Bit Long—Tale About RI History." *Providence Journal*, January 16, 2011.

"If we are not much mistaken…" *Providence Journal*, January 8, 1844.

"John Gordon was executed…" *Providence Journal*, February 15, 1845.

Kennedy, Meri R. "John Gordon Gets His Final Rest." Cranston Herald, September 14, 2011.

Kulgus, Laura. "Taking the State: The Murder Trial of John Gordon." *Rhode Island Catholic*, February 3, 2011.

Maguire, Kara. "Judge, Jury, and Executioner: The Gordon Trial. Providence, RI, 1844." Thesis. n.d.

"Most Atrocious Murder." *Providence Journal*, January 1, 1844.

"Murder of Mr. Sprague." *Providence Journal*, January 2, 1844.

"Resignation of Mr. Sprague." *Providence Journal*, January 17, 1844.

"State's Last Executed Man Finally Gets a Proper Burial." *Cranston Patch*. n.d.

"Supreme Court." *Providence Journal*, March 28, 1844.

"Supreme Court." *Providence Journal*, April 20, 1844.

"Trial of the Gordons." *Providence Journal*, April 18, 1844.

"Trial of the Gordons." *Providence Journal*, April 19, 1844.

Wyss, Bob. "They Did Not Know What They Were Doing." *Providence Journal*, July 19, 1981.

Manuscripts

Dooley, Ken. *The Murder Trial of John Gordon*. Cranston, 2010

INDEX

About the Author

Paul F. Caranci is a third-generation resident of North Providence and has been a student of history for many years. With his wife, Margie, he founded the Municipal Heritage Group in 2009. He is also on the board of directors of the Heritage Harbor Museum and the Rhode Island Heritage Hall of Fame. Paul has served as Rhode Island's deputy secretary of state since 2007 and has been elected to the North Providence Town Council, where he served from 1994 to 2010. He has a bachelor's degree in political science from Providence College and is currently enrolled in the master's program at Roger Williams University. He has two children, Heather and Matthew, and four grandchildren: Matthew, Jacob, Vincent and Casey. This is Paul's second book. The History Press published *North Providence: A History & the People Who Shaped It* in 2012.